Social Security Law in the Czech Republic

Social Security Law in the Czech Republic

Kristina Koldinská
Roman Lang

This book was originally published as a monograph in the International Encyclopaedia of Laws/Social Security Law.

Founding Editor: Roger Blanpain
General Editor: Frank Hendrickx
Volume Editor: Willy van Eeckhoutte

Wolters Kluwer

Published by:
Kluwer Law International B.V.
PO Box 316
2400 AH Alphen aan den Rijn
The Netherlands
E-mail: international-sales@wolterskluwer.com
Website: lrus.wolterskluwer.com

Sold and distributed in North, Central and South America by:
Wolters Kluwer Legal & Regulatory U.S.
7201 McKinney Circle
Frederick, MD 21704
United States of America
Email: customer.service@wolterskluwer.com

Sold and distributed in all other countries by:
Air Business Subscriptions
Rockwood House
Haywards Heath
West Sussex
RH16 3DH
United Kingdom
Email: international-customerservice@wolterskluwer.com

Printed on acid-free paper

ISBN 978-94-035-1875-6

e-Book: ISBN 978-94-035-1901-2
web-PDF: ISBN 978-94-035-1913-5

Printed in the United Kingdom.

The Authors

Kristina Koldinská is an associate professor at the Charles University Faculty of Law. Since 1997, she has been working at the Department of Labour Law and Social Law, where she teaches Social Security Saw and Labour Law. She also teaches courses on Migration and Social Law and Discrimination and Social Law, both in European and international context. She publishes extensively in Czech Republic as well as with various foreign publishing houses and legal reviews. Her research interests include gender equality, EU social law, coordination of social security and social assistance. She is a member of Commission's Network of legal experts in the field of antidiscrimination and of MoveS, a network on free movement of workers and coordination of social security. Both are long-lasting projects run by prestigious European universities and financed by the EU Commission.

The work of Kristina Koldinská on this chapter has been kindly supported by the Czech Science Foundation – GACR through its project N. 17-03398S 'The International Labour Organisation and its role in the development of social law in Europe'.

Roman Lang (born 1982) studied Law at Charles University in Prague (2000–2005). After graduation in 2005, he began working in the Czech Social Security Administration, department of methodology, as lawyer-specialist in the field of pension insurance, where he worked until the year 2012. Since the year 2006, he has been working as Lecturer in Labour Law and Social Security Law at the Faculty of Law, Charles University, Prague. In 2009, he obtained the post-graduate degree (PhD) after the defence of his dissertation thesis 'Claims for compensation of participants in national revolts in Czechoslovak and Czech Social Security Law'. During his doctoral study (2007–2008), he spent one semester by the study stay-in Wales on Cardiff University, Faculty of Law. Since 2007, Roman Lang has been giving lessons in several private educational institutions (agencies) dealing with the people's retraining or deepening of their qualification – there he teaches the Law of Pension Insurance, especially the statutory duties of employers in this field of law. Since 2011, he has also been working in law office (attorney JUDr. Tomas Pelikan,

Prague) as the main consultant in the matters of labour law. Since 2012, he has been working in the Ministry of Labour and Social Affairs, department of pension insurance. Apart from his pedagogical and scientific activities, Roman Lang publishes regularly articles in Czech and foreign research journals and other publications.

Table of Contents

Table of Contents

List of Abbreviations

Coll.	Collection of Laws
CZK	Czech Crown
CSSA	Czech Social Security Administration
DSSA	District Social Security Administration
ECHR	European Court of Human Rights
RBLO	Regional Branches of the Labour Office of the Czech Republic
TIW	Temporary Incapacity to Work

List of Abbreviations

General Introduction

§1. General Background

1. The Czech Republic (*Česká republika*) is a constitutional parliamentary democracy established in 1993 when the Czech and Slovak Federation (Czechoslovakia) peacefully separated into two independent states, the Czech Republic and Slovakia. The country lies in Central Europe to the southeast of Germany. Measuring 78,866 square kilometres, the landlocked Czech Republic is bordered by Germany, Poland, Slovakia and Austria.

2. According to figures from the national census, 10,562,214 inhabitants were living in the Czech Republic in spring 2011; which means that Czech society increased in numbers by some 3% during the last ten years. Behind this increase is not only the increasing birth rate of the last few years but also, primarily, the immigration of foreigners (coming mainly from Ukraine, Slovakia, Vietnam, Russia, Germany and Poland), who number almost half a million.

3. At the same time, Czech society is growing older. While the number of people of working age has increased during these ten years by almost 200,000, the number of people aged 65 and above increased by as much as 260,000. Meanwhile, the number of children aged 14 and under has been constantly decreasing since the 1980s, as has their share in the total population.

4. All of the above places a great demand on social security, especially on pension insurance.

§2. Historical Background

5. The origin of modern systems of social security in Czechoslovakia is to be found in the Austro-Hungarian Monarchy, in the nineteenth century. The social assistance system was established in the 1850s, and at the end of the century, social insurance was introduced through so-called Taafe's reform, which was strongly inspired by Bismarkian social reforms in Germany.

6. Soon after the birth of the independent Czechoslovak Republic in 1918, there emerged calls for changes which would not only improve the system of benefits but also eliminate the persisting dispersed organization. Substantial modifications were introduced by Act No. 268/1919 Collection of Laws (Coll.), which abolished association sickness funds with less than 400 members, and enterprise sickness funds (with the exception of those for railway, navigation and some state enterprises), and forbade their further establishment. Corporation sickness funds, with less than 1,000 members, were deprived of the right to provide insurance with legal effect. This measure still left 517 sickness funds in existence. At that time, sickness insurance applied to all persons performing work or services on the basis of employment, service or apprenticeship relationships.

7. A very important piece of law was adopted through Act No. 221/1924 Coll., which entered into force on 1 July 1926. This Act not only introduced disability and old-age insurance for workers but also, in particular, unified a system of social insurance which had become very fragmented by then. From the point of view of social policy and insurance mathematics, this was a real masterpiece of early Czechoslovak legislation.[1] The disability and old-age insurance were entrusted to the Central Social Insurance Office, which also acquired the right to intervene in internal affairs of district sickness insurance offices, to manage and to supervise them. In spite of that, the sickness insurance offices remained autonomous legal persons, the operations of which were governed by their statutes. Thus, the sickness insurance offices were the most important organizations of social insurance in Czechoslovakia before the Second World War. Apart from the sickness insurance offices and the Central Social Insurance Office, there was also the General Pensions Institute, the organization for old-age insurance for private employees of executive rank.

8. High standards and a tendency towards further unification of the social insurance system in the Czechoslovak Republic persisted after the Second World War also. Act No. 99/1948 Coll. on National Insurance, unified sickness insurance and old-age insurance, abolished all carriers of sickness, old-age, disability and pension insurance, and appointed the Central National Insurance Office as their legal successor to acquire all their property. This Act was seen as a great success in terms of collaboration between scientists and social politicians, both of those who had remained in the country and those who had been in exile in the United Kingdom during the war.

9. Generally speaking, the insurance system at that time can be characterized as follows:

– Insurance covered not only wage-earners but also pensioners and the unemployed; contributions amounted to 6.8% (health insurance) and 10% (old-age pension) of the base (sum of income); these were paid by the employer on behalf of the employees; self-employed entrepreneurs paid 16.7% for themselves and

1. About the history and role of this act *see, e.g.*, Tomeš, I. 80 let sociálního pojištění (80 years of social insurance). Praha 2005, available at http://www.cssz.cz/stranky/konference-80let/prispevky.htm#tomes1 (accessed 13 Jul. 2016).

cooperating members of their families. The state contributed the so-called summary contribution to health insurance for pensioners and the unemployed, paid 50% of the costs of medical care provided in public institutions and contributed to old-age insurance.

- Sickness insurance provided benefits in kind (healthcare) and pecuniary (cash) benefits (sickness benefits).
- The national insurance framework also developed forms of old-age insurance and general care of beneficiaries and their dependents.

10. In the 1950s, this system of comprehensive social insurance was replaced with the social security system. The traditional social insurance administration was brought to a definite end by Act No. 102/1951 Coll. on the Reconstruction of National Insurance, which converted the revenue and expenditure of health and pension insurance into parts of the state budget. The changes which took place in the years to follow can be characterized as follows:

- In 1952, pension insurance was separated and the State Social Security Office was established.
- Health insurance (benefits in kind) was abolished and replaced with healthcare in health service districts.
- Sickness insurance was taken over by trade unions (administration and financing) and enterprises (implementation).

11. The whole system was centralized and followed the Soviet model of social security. During the 1950s and 1960s, all the private areas of social security – including the system of social assistance – were abolished; social security as such was run by the state and its institutions (including also social services); and the citizen was only socially secured by the state, regardless of her/his contribution to social welfare.

12. Important changes took place in 1956 with the adoption of the new Act on sickness insurance of employees (Act No. 54/1956 Coll.), and the new Act on social security (Act No. 55/1956 Coll.). The social security entitlements of the members of cooperatives (production and agricultural) and self-employed persons were regulated by government orders. While these regulations were in effect, the costs of the whole social security system rose steeply, so that until the early 1990s the costs of social security became unbearable for the not-so-ample state budget.

13. Further revision of the social security legislation in 1964 (Act No. 101/1964 and Act No. 103/1964 Coll.) differed from all post-war predecessors and made a break from the development trend of that time. The reform in 1964 was also very important because Czechoslovakia became a socialist federation. In 1966, Act No. 20/1966 Coll. on Public Health, introduced the so-called free medical service (state system), and in 1968 a new modification of maternity benefits (benefits introduced in order to provide mothers caring for small children something similar to a 'social loan', and to compensate for their staying at home without the possibility to work) and children's allowances were adopted (Act No. 88/1968 Coll.). Further, changes in the organization and implementation of health insurance and social security were made through the introduction of financing on federal and republican levels.

14. The reforms of the social security system carried out in the 1970s and 1980s (Act No. 121/1975 Coll. and Act No. 100/1988 Coll.) endeavoured to create a more favourable impression on the population through a more distinct social policy, aimed especially at families with small children, in order to encourage a population increase (the so-called Husak's pro-nativity policy). These modifications, however, did not remedy any of the fundamental shortcomings of the system. Moreover, the economic problems of the 1980s forced the government to adopt a soberer social security policy.

15. For decades the social security system had been based on the principles of state social security paid directly from the state budget. This system was marked by a static character which prevented it from reacting adequately to the development of wages and prices or procuring the required financial and material resources in sufficient time. Typical of this system was the so-called residual method for the solution of social problems, i.e., redistributing funds only after some have been left over.[2]

16. Shortly after political changes in November 1989 – still in former Czechoslovakia – economic reform was commenced, accompanied by an extensive and fundamental reform of the legal system. In the framework of this process, a programme of social reform was also prepared. In fact, on the same day that the so-called scenario of economic reform was presented, the 'scenario of social reform' was proposed as well. This was a very important sign that economic reform could not be performed successfully without social reform.

17. The new concept of social security (introduced gradually after 1989) represents a transition from state paternalism to the participation and responsibility of citizens and social groups for their social situation and future. It is based on the principle that citizens and families must ensure the widest possible scope of their needs on a socially acceptable level through their own efforts. The state should interfere only where the citizen or the family cannot manage, for subjective or objective reasons. The state, however, must guarantee citizens' security on a dignified level, as many sources of international and European law on fundamental social rights provide.

18. As early as the first half of 1990, the necessary prerequisites for social reform were created by the unification of social security legislation, which on the one hand equalized the status of all persons performing gainful activities (before,

2. Further about the history of social policy in the twentieth century, *see* Rákosník, J., Tomeš, I. (eds.). Sociální stát v Československu. Právně-institucionální vývoj v letech 1918-1992. Praha, Auditorium 2012.

workers had been divided into several categories, with manual workers and members of the communist party as the most privileged group); on the other hand, established new social security administration bodies no longer dependent on state central power.

19. Social security reform started first with the social insurance system, where the principle of social insurance and contributions to it had to be reintroduced (during the socialist era, the whole social security system, including social insurance, had been financed by taxes).

20. At the same time, the new functioning of the health services had to be established (until then, it had been centralized, administrated by the state and not financed by contributions) and so *health insurance* was also introduced (following, to a certain extent, the German model). Three new acts on health insurance were adopted at the end of 1991 and completed by the Act on contributions to general health insurance in 1992. As of the same year, it was also made possible to establish private health insurance companies. The purpose and meaning of health insurance is the payment of the costs of healthcare provided to beneficiaries. The appropriate health insurance companies (General Health Insurance Company of the Czech Republic and other private employees' health insurance companies), thus, make payments for healthcare provided to their beneficiaries on the basis of public health insurance, according to the contracts concluded with medical institutions. Rules for providing healthcare services were reformed as late as in 2012 – through the Acts No. 372/2011 Coll. on health services, No. 373/2011 Coll. on special health services and No. 374/2011 Coll. on emergency medical service, which replaced the old Act No. 20/1966 Coll. on care for the health of people.

21. The same applies also to *social security contributions* as well as to contributions to the state employment policy (the first step to unemployment insurance), the payment (into the account of the Czech Social Security Administration (CSSA)) of which also started on 1 January 1993, without the introduction of the insurance itself. For the time being, these contributions form part of the revenue of the state budget from which social security costs are also funded. Social insurance is financed primarily from contributions paid according to the Act on social security insurance and contributions to state employment policy (Act No. 589/1992 Coll., as amended), by employees, employers and self-employed persons.

22. Since 1996, pension insurance contributions, however, have been kept in a special state budget account and formed an autonomous income item of the state budget (section 2 of Act of the Czech National Council No. 589/1992 Coll., as amended). According to the Budget Rules of the Czech Republic (Act No. 218/2000 Coll. on Budget Rules and Amendments of some Related Acts), the difference between the revenue from insurance contributions and expenditure on pension insurance benefits forms a part of state financial assets. The funds in this account may be used only for pension valorization and to cover the negative balance of the insurance account.

23. Until the current time, the principal reform steps in social security administration have not yet been taken, and only partial changes have been made in the field of financing. In order to reform the system of administration of social insurance, a bill was submitted in the middle of 2000, on the basis of which the Social Insurance Company had to be established to take over the management of social insurance from the CSSA. Social insurance financing would have had to have been totally severed from the state budget. However, the bill did not make it through the Chamber of Deputies of the Parliament of the Czech Republic, and no other attempt in this direction has been taken since then.

24. Sickness insurance, which provides security to citizens in case of social events, through short-term benefits (sickness benefit, care allowance – support of wage-earners taking care of a sick member of the family, wage compensation during pregnancy and maternity, and pecuniary assistance during maternity – which can be claimed also by fathers, under certain conditions), also underwent some reform changes. As the system had previously also comprised of some state-funded benefits for children and families (not insurance benefits), it was necessary to eliminate these benefits from the sickness insurance system, which occurred in 1995 through the Act on State Social Support (Act No. 117/1995 Coll.), and related Act No. 118/1995 Coll. (amending and supplementing some Acts in connection with the adoption of the State Social Support Act). Another important reform of sickness insurance took place in 2006, through the adoption of a new Act, Act No. 187/2006 Coll. on sickness insurance. Very important and 'revolutionary' changes were brought to the sickness insurance system by Act No. 148/2017 Coll. (effective from 1 February 2018) and by Act No. 310/2017 Coll. (effective from 1 June 2018) – after decades of its existence, the number of benefits increased from four to six. Two new benefits – paternity allowance and long-term care allowance – were introduced.

25. Reform of the *pension system* formed an integral part of the transformation of the whole social security system. The present pension system, introduced in 1995 by the Pension Insurance Act (Act No. 155/1995 Coll.), is conceived as an obligatory system guaranteed by the state. The insurance secures citizens in case of old age, disability and/or death of a breadwinner, through long-term benefits (individual types of pensions). As early as in 1994, the third pillar of pensions was established (Act No. 42/1994 Coll. on state-contributory supplementary pension insurance). Recently, the system was subjected to decisive changes – in 2011, the system of pension savings was introduced by Act No. 426/2011 Coll. on pension savings. As early as in 2016, the system was, however, de facto abolished and all contributions were paid out or transferred to a private system of supplementary pension savings (Act No. 427/2011 Coll. on supplementary pension savings), which de facto replaced the previous state-contributory supplementary pension insurance. The main reason for abolishing the system of pension savings was the fact that there were too few people participating in this system (80,000 participants, whereas 500,000 participants were expected). This situation was caused by quite a strong negative campaign against the system of pension savings, which was introduced without political consensus.

26. Post-1989, another newly conceived system is the system of *state social support*. With state social support benefits, the state contributes, in cases of social events defined by the Act, to the coverage of subsistence costs and other basic personal needs of children and families, and grants this support also in case of some other social events (increase of housing costs, costs related to childbirth, expenses for funeral services, etc.). Since January 1996, some fundamental state social support benefits (such as children's allowance) have been granted dependent on the net family income or on the condition that the family income does not exceed a certain limit specified by the Act. These benefits also included childbirth grants and funeral allowances.

27. The different concept of the newly conceived social security system also comprises of fundamental changes in the field of *social assistance*. Its qualitatively new content is also manifested by the substitution of the term 'social assistance' for the formerly used term 'social care'. The purpose of social assistance is to ensure basic living necessities to citizens in a difficult social situation who are unable to meet these needs through their own efforts or with the assistance of their family. The new system of social assistance was introduced, as late as, in 2006 when Act No. 111/2006 Coll. on aid in material need and Act No. 108/2006 Coll. on social services were adopted. The very old and no longer well-functioning system of social care was abolished as of 2012 with the introduction of Act No. 329/2011 Coll. on provision of subsidies to people with disabilities. Social assistance as such is focused on the elderly, people with disabilities, socially excluded groups and families with children facing certain social or health difficulties, etc. The main scope of social assistance is to prevent as much social exclusion as possible, and where social exclusion occurs, to activate instruments encouraging social inclusion as effectively as possible. The system also contains many motivational measures in order to help people to solve their situations by themselves where possible.

28. In order to be exhaustive, it should be also mentioned that in 2006, Act No. 266/2006 Coll. on accident insurance, was adopted. This Act, which never entered into force, envisaged the establishment of a new system of accident insurance run by the CSSA. Employers should have contributed substantially to this system, and in case of work accidents, several benefits could have been claimed by the worker. This Act never entered into force and was abolished in 2015 by Act No. 205/2015 Coll., which returned accident insurance where it was before – to the Labour Code (Act No. 262/2006 Coll., Labour Code). It is based on the principle of objective liability of the employer for damage to the employee caused by an industrial accident or due to an occupational disease, with obligatory commercial insurance of statutory liability for damages.

It shall also be mentioned that, as of 1 January 2016, the long-awaited Civil Service Act (Act No. 234/2014 Coll.) entered into force. This Act provides for some specific ways of social security for civil servants, namely in the field of sickness insurance, accidents at work and harmonizing work and family life.[3]

3. Commentary to this law, Pichrt, J. (edt.) Civil Service Act. Wolters Kluwer. Prague 2015.

§3. SOURCES OF SOCIAL SECURITY LAW

I. General

29. In the Czech Republic, the sources of social security law include legal norms and other legal instruments formulating the rights and obligations of certain subjects. Their purpose is to prevent or eliminate difficult social situations of citizens. These rights and obligations are implemented in legal social security relations.

30. In the field of social security law, normative legal acts represent the most common sources of law. A source of law also represents international agreements on social security.[4]

31. With reference to the domestic legal liability of international treaties binding on the Czech Republic, it is necessary to point out that promulgated international treaties, the ratification of which is approved by the Parliament of the Czech Republic, form a component of state legislation. These treaties are directly binding and are superior to domestic laws. Article 10 of the Constitution of the Czech Republic affords these international treaties with a higher legal force than domestic laws, which is also significant for the interpretation of domestic laws. Such treaties must be promulgated in the Collection of Laws (Coll.) and, since 1 January 2000, in the Collection of International Treaties. On the day of promulgation, they become a direct source of Czech law.

32. The subjective right to social security in the territory of the Czech Republic is declared in the Charter of Fundamental Rights and Freedoms promulgated by Resolution of the Presidium of the Czech National Council No. 2/1993 Coll., as a component part of the constitutional system of the Czech Republic (particularly Articles 30 through 32),[5] and in international covenants and treaties ratified by the Czech Republic (in particular the International Covenant on Economic, Social and Cultural Rights, promulgated under No. 120/1976 Coll., and the Conventions of the International Labour Organization Nos 102 (1952), 128 (1967), 130 (1969), 167 (1988), etc.). The European Social Charter adopted in 1961 by the then Member States of the Council of Europe was ratified by the Czech Republic as late as in 2000 and published under No. 14/2000, Collection of International Treaties, whereas the European Social Security Code had to wait even longer – it was adopted in 2001 under No. 90/2001, Collection of International Treaties.

---

4. A list of bilateral agreements on social security, where one of the parties is the Czech Republic, is available at http://www.cssz.cz/cz/mezinarodni-smlouvy/smlouvy-uzavrene-cr/prehled-smluv.htm (accessed 13 Jul. 2016).
5. On interpretation of social rights by the Czech Constitutional Court, *see* Pichrt, J., Koldinská, K. Czech Republic. In: ILO The Right to Social Security in the European Constitutions. ILO Geneva.

33. Last but not least, European Union (EU) law also represents an integrated part of the Czech legal system, and so several parts of EU primary law and also regulations and directives form a source of law regulating social security or social law issues.

34. The conditions under which a citizen may claim her/his constitutional right to social security and the forms in which she/he is granted social security are set out in implementing acts (*see* below section II). These acts defining the individual forms of social security provide, as a rule: the form of security, personal and material scope, conditions of entitlement origin and duration, the means and level of security (amount of benefits), means of funding, decision-making (benefits procedure and procedures in other matters) and administration.

35. Details and specific conditions connected with the implementation of the acts are entrusted to the government. Also, the process of benefit valorization, dependent on the increase in prices or wages or the costs of living, is entrusted to the government which should make the appropriate modifications in the form of government orders (*see* below section III).

36. The assurance of social security is entrusted to the respective state administration authorities (Ministry of Labour and Social Affairs, CSSA, Ministry of Health or Ministry of Finance, as a rule). Czech social security system is also run by private subjects (e.g., health insurance companies, pension companies, private providers of healthcare), as well as by regional branches of the Labour Office and local authorities (regions or local communities).

II. Legislation (Laws)

37. Below, we list the most important acts which are generally binding regulations in the field of social security. These acts are quoted under their initial number and year of issue in the Collection of Laws with the understanding that they are to be considered 'as amended'.

Health Insurance

- Act No. 48/1997 Coll. on public health insurance and amendments and supplements of some related Acts.
- Act of the Czech National Council No. 551/1991 Coll. on the General Health Insurance Company of the Czech Republic.
- Act of the Czech National Council No. 280/1992 Coll. on sector, branch, enterprise and other health insurance companies.
- Act of the Czech National Council No. 592/1992 Coll. on contributions to general health insurance.
- Act No. 372/2011 Coll. on healthcare services.
- Act No. 373/2011 Coll. on specific healthcare services.
- Act No. 374/2011 Coll. on healthcare rescue and emergency services.

- Act No. 258/2000 Coll. on the protection of public health.

Sickness Insurance

- Act No. 187/2006 Coll. on sickness insurance.
- Act No. 589/1992 Coll. on contributions to social security and contributions to state employment policy.

Pension Insurance

- Act No. 155/1995 Coll. on pension insurance.
- Act of the Czech National Council No. 582/1991 Coll. on social security organization and implementation.
- Act No. 589/1992 Coll. on contributions to social security and contributions to state employment policy.
- Act No. 427/2011 Coll. on supplementary pension savings.
- Act No. 42/1994 Coll. on supplementary pension insurance with state contribution.
- Act No. 376/2015 Coll. on termination of the pension savings.

Industrial Accidents and Occupational Diseases

- Act No. 262/2006 Coll. the Labour Code.
- Act No. 234/2014 Coll. on civil service
- Act No. 155/1995 Coll. on pension insurance.
- Act No. 251/2005 Coll. on work inspection.
- Act No. 89/2012 Coll. the Civil Code.

Unemployment

- Act No. 435/2004 Coll. on employment.
- Act No. 118/2000 Coll. on employees' protection in case of an employer's insolvency, and the amendments of some Acts.

State Social Support

- Act No. 117/1995 Coll. on state social support.
- Act No. 110/2006 Coll. on subsistence and the living minimum.

Social Assistance

- Act No. 111/2006 Coll. on social aid in material need.
- Act No. 108/2006 Coll. on social services.
- Act No. 329/2001 Coll. on the provision of subsidies to people with disabilities.
- Act No. 110/2006 Coll. on subsistence and the living minimum.

III. Regulations (Orders and Ordinances)

38. This part comprises of some important, generally binding regulations from the field of social security. These have the form of orders of the government or are issued as ordinances by the respective central state administration authorities (ministries). In both forms, they are of the character of regulations implementing the respective acts. Also, these sub-statutory regulations should be considered 'as amended'.

Health Insurance

- Ordinance of the Ministry of Health No. 134/1998 Coll. issuing the list of medical services with their point values.
- Ordinance of the Ministry of Health No. 618/2006 Coll. issuing framework contracts for healthcare providers.

Pension Insurance

- Ordinance of the Ministry of Labour and Social Affairs No. 284/1995 Coll. to administer the Act on pension insurance.
- Ordinance of the Ministry of Labour and Social Affairs No. 359/2009 Coll. laying down the percentage decline in the ability to work and essentials of a report on disability and regulating the assessment of working capacity for disability.
- Order of the Government No. 363/2009 Coll. laying down the retiring age and the recalculation of old-age pensions of some groups of mineworkers who began to perform their occupation before 1993.
- Order of the Government No. 141/2013 Coll. laying down the more detailed regulation of mutual transfer of pension rights in relation to the pension system of the European Union.
- Order of the Government No. 343/2017 Coll. laying down the amount of general calculation base per year 2016, coefficient for indexation of the general calculation base per year 2016, reduction levels for calculation of the computational base for the year 2018, basic component of pensions laid down for the year 2018 and valorization of pensions in the year 2018.

Industrial Accidents and Occupational Diseases

- Order of the Government No. 67/2005 Coll. on the modification of compensation of the loss of earnings after the cessation of incapacity to work due to an industrial accident or an occupational disease, on modification of compensation for survivors' subsistence costs, and on the modification of the compensation of the loss of earnings after the cessation of incapacity to work or in case of disability (modification of the compensation).
- Order of the Government No. 329/2005 Coll. on modification of compensation for loss of earnings after the cessation of work, incapacity or invalidity caused by injury during service or due to an occupational disease affecting soldiers in the course of basic military or civilian service, as well as during the execution of military training, and on the modification of compensations for loss of wages after the cessation of work, incapacity or invalidity caused by injury during service or an occupational disease affecting professional soldiers (modification of compensation of loss of earnings of soldiers).
- Ordinance of the Ministry of Finance No. 125/1993 Coll. defining conditions and rates of statutory insurance of employer's liability for damages due to an industrial accident or an occupational disease (which is in force only until Act No. 266/2006 Coll. enters into force – which should be as of 1 January 2013).

Unemployment

- Order of the Government No. 515/2004 Coll. on material support for new job generation and employees' material support during the process of their retraining or education in the framework of investment incentives.
- Ordinance of the Ministry of Labour and Social Affairs No. 518/2004 Coll. by means of which Act No. 435/2004 Coll. on employment is introduced.
- Ordinance of the Ministry of Labour and Social Affairs No. 519/2004 Coll. on the retraining of job applicants and job seekers and on the retraining of employees.
- Order of the Government No. 64/2009 Coll. on the setting of kinds of work which cannot be intermediated by an employment agency in the form of temporary assignment of an employee to the work performance by an employer.
- Ordinance of the Ministry of Education, Youth and Sports and of the Ministry of Labour and Social Affairs No. 176/2009 Coll. on the setting of proprieties of application for accreditation of educational programmes, organization of education in retraining facility and the way of its termination.
- Ordinance of the Ministry of Labour and Social Affairs No. 322/2017 Coll. on the setting of a list of employment branches which include seasonal activities.
- Ordinance of the Ministry of Labour and Social Affairs No. 346/2017 Coll. on the binding schedule of the certificate of a job seeker's incapacity to fulfil his duties by reason of illness or injury and on the binding schedule of the certificate of a job seeker's examination in healthcare facility.
- Notification of the Ministry of Labour and Social Affairs No. 447/2017 Coll. on the announcement of the average wage in the national economy within the first three quarters of the year 2017 for the purposes of the Employment Act.

Social Assistance

- Ordinance of the Ministry of Labour and Social Affairs No. 388/2011 Coll. on implementing some provisions of the act on providing benefits to persons with disabilities.
- Ordinance of the Ministry of Labour and Social Affairs No. 505/2006 Coll. on implementing some provisions of the Act on Social Services.
- Ordinance of the Ministry of Labour and Social Affairs No. 389/2011 Coll. on implementing some provisions of the Act on aid in material need.

IV. Adjudications

39. In contrast to the Anglo-Saxon legal system, in the Czech Republic judicial decisions do not become precedents and, therefore, are not a formal source of law. Decisions of courts within the administrative judiciary (there being no special social judiciary), particularly those published regularly in the Collection of Judicial Decisions and Standpoints, however, have become an important determinant of interpretation and application of social security law. The legal interpretation of higher courts is binding for lower courts.

40. The assertion of substantive rights and legally protected interests and obligations of the legal subjects is assured by the norms of adjective law, ranging from general administrative procedure, codified by Act No. 500/2004 Coll. on Rules of Administrative Procedure to special administrative procedure, providing a different procedure of administrative authorities to administrative proceedings involving the judicial review of administrative decisions. The administrative judiciary, within which the courts ensure the protection of public subjective rights of natural and legal persons, is defined by Act No. 150/2002 Coll. on Rules of Administrative Judiciary. Through this Act, the Supreme Administrative Court was established as was expressly provided for in the Constitution (Article 91, paragraph 1 of the Constitution of the Czech Republic, Act No. 1/1993 Coll.).

41. The relation of the Rules of Administrative Procedure – concerning both old and/or new versions – to the Rules of Administrative Judiciary depends on the limits of considerations of the administrative court in the process of review of administrative decisions, namely if any substantial violation of rules with regard to procedure at the administrative office happened and if, at the same time, the intensity of such violation of procedure might have caused an unlawful decision of the administrative body with regard to the relevant matter. In such a case, due to administrative procedure failures, the court is expressly obliged to act in harmony with the legislator's indication in section 76, paragraph 1, letter c of the Rules of Administrative Judiciary and must revoke the disputed decision. The case law of the administrative courts, namely that published in the Collection of Decisions of the Supreme Administrative Court, substantially influences procedures and the decision-making practice of administrative courts and administrative offices and enables the unification of the process. Since it was established, the Supreme Administrative Court has gained a great moral authority within the judicial system and also among lawyers.

42. Another noteworthy instrument of judicial protection regarding the routine of administrative offices, especially in the case of their potential inactivity, is the possibility to lodge an appeal with the administrative court, such that the relevant administrative office is ordered to issue its decision on the subject matter or issue a certificate. The objective is to provide protection of eligibility of a public quality level, even if the result of the administrative decision concerns an evaluation of private legal rights.

43. Thus, social security matters can be handled, both, through the administrative procedure and by judicial review, possibly by a combination of both procedures, depending on the concrete case type. The purpose of court procedure is to enable the examination of the material correctness of the decision issued by an administrative body, namely with reference to Article 36, paragraph 2 of the Charter of Fundamental Rights and Freedoms, as well as Article 4 of the Constitution of the Czech Republic, substantiating the necessity of judicial protection in the field of social security also.

44. As entitlement to social benefits ranks among the constitutionally guaranteed rights of citizens (Article 30 of the Charter of Fundamental Rights and Freedoms), it must be fully subject to judicial review. For this reason, the legislation provides that in matters of sickness insurance it is always possible to submit a remedy to the court against any decision of the social security body.

45. Also, all decisions of the insurance carrier concerning pension benefits are subject to judicial review, after being examined under administrative review (so-called objections – *see* below Part VIII on pensions). With regard to the serious character of social claims of beneficiaries and to facilitate the implementation of these claims, it is prescribed expressly that beneficiaries do not have to cover the insurance carrier's procedural expenses in social insurance matters at all, including the costs of court proceedings. The remedial procedure in matters concerning state social support proceeds first along administrative and only, subsequently, along judicial review lines.

46. Any appeal lodged has the quality of initiation of a judicial enquiry in the case that all acceptable legitimate notices of appeal under administrative procedure have failed. A submitted appeal does not have any dilatory effect, but the court can assign the appeal such dilatory effect based on the claimant's suggestion, especially in cases where the execution or any other legal consequences may cause unavoidable harm to the claimant.

47. If the court finds that the appeal was reasonable, it will cancel the disputed decision due to unlawfulness or in consequence of procedural failures, and return the matter to the administrative body which has been challenged. If the court finds the appeal unreasonable, it will reject it.

48. The quality of notice of appeal against a valid decision of a regional court equates to a cassation appeal which can be submitted within a maximum of two weeks after the delivery of the decision of the regional court, namely to the same court; the term is also preserved if the cassation appeal is submitted directly to the Supreme Administrative Court, which is responsible for the proceedings thereof. It is the obligation of the claimant to be represented by an attorney with the exception of cases where she/he or the person representing her/him has a university law education as required for the performance of the functions of an attorney.

49. Apart from the decision-making practice of courts within the administrative judiciary, the findings of the Constitutional Court are also of considerable significance. The role of this court is to interpret the Constitution and to define criteria for the solution of possible conflicts of fundamental rights and freedoms, i.e., to specify the conditions under which one right or freedom has priority over other rights and freedoms. Under Act No. 182/1993 Coll. on the Constitutional Court, certain findings, in particular, those abolishing the provisions of acts or sub-statutory regulations, are published in the Collection of Laws. The Constitutional Court of the Czech Republic has issued a number of decisions in the field of social security, solving some important issues.

V. Labour Contracts

50. Social security law is an autonomous branch of Czech law. In its nature and purpose, it is a public law as opposed to labour law, which is a private law with certain elements of public law. Individual labour contracts or collective agreements may contain an obligation of the employer to contribute to a state-contributed supplementary pension or supplementary pension savings of own employees (according to Act No. 427/2011 Coll.). Such a contribution must respect the principle of equal treatment guaranteed by the Antidiscrimination Act (Act No. 198/2009 Coll.)

51. Apart from wage and labour law claims, collective agreements also regulate some social issues. Thus, for example, the collective agreement may provide higher than statutory amounts of ad hoc indemnity for the spouse, children and possibly also parents of an employee who has died as a result of an industrial accident or an occupational disease.

52. Technical and procedural aspects of collective bargaining and detailed conditions of the conclusion of collective agreements are codified, together with further issues (settlement of labour disputes and use of extreme means to pursue labour rights, such as strikes and lockouts) by Act No. 2/1991 Coll. on collective bargaining. This Act also codifies sickness and social security claims during a strike (section 24) or lockout (section 30, paragraph 3 of the above-mentioned Act).

53. Under this Act, collective agreements in the Czech Republic are of two types. On the one hand, there are higher-order collective agreements concluded by trade union organizations with more than two employers, or by trade union associations with the employers' organization(s). Their content is usually based on the results of the negotiations of the Council of Economic and Social Agreement as a tripartite body. On the other hand, another type of collective agreements are enterprise collective agreements which are concluded between the respective trade union body and the employer.

Part I. The Institutions

Chapter 1. Public Institutions

§1. Ministerial Departments

54. Legal regulations codifying the organization of social security contain no umbrella term which would cover all institutions ensuring the implementation of the rights and obligations arising from legal relations in the field of social security. The term most frequently used in these regulations is 'social security bodies'. This term is defined in section 3 of the Act of the Czech National Council No. 582/1991 Coll. on social security organization and implementation, as amended. According to its provisions, the number of social security bodies includes not only ministries but also some other public institutions, such as the:

- Ministry of Labour and Social Affairs;
- CSSA;
- District Social Security Administrations (DSSA);
- Ministry of Interior;
- Ministry of Justice; and
- Ministry of Defence.

55. According to the above-mentioned Act, social security bodies are state institutions, the primary task of which is the settlement of benefit claims arising from legal relations of sickness insurance and pension insurance.

56. In accordance with the above-mentioned Act, we can define the competence of the Ministry of Labour and Social Affairs as follows:

- management and control of the exercise of state administration in the field of social security;
- assurance of tasks connected with the further development of social security;
- assurance of tasks arising from international treaties in the field of social security;
- management of the CSSA;
- inspections concerning health conditions and citizens' working ability for the purpose of judicial review proceedings in matters of pension insurance;
- possible establishment and administration of social institutions and institutes providing diagnostic service; and

– supervision of the provision of social services by organizations and citizens and the imposition of measures to remedy ascertained shortcomings.

57. The Minister of Labour and Social Affairs may remedy undue hardships which may arise from the implementation of social security and may authorize the social security administrations to remedy undue hardships in individual cases.

58. The Ministries of Defence, the Interior and Justice manage, control and implement the pension insurance of professional soldiers through their own bodies, members of the Czech police and members of the Penitentiary Service of the Czech Republic, within their respective competence. Their bodies decide, within their competence, on the pension insurance benefits of the aforementioned persons and pay these benefits to those persons. Within their competence, the Ministers of Defence, the Interior and Justice may remedy undue hardships which may arise during the implementation of social security concerning members of the respective armed forces.

§2. Public Institutions

59. A specific position is accorded to the CSSA. This social security body, with district offices, administers pension insurance and sickness insurance. In the case of appeal regarding sickness insurance, the CSSA is also an appeal institution.

60. Moreover, the CSSA collects all contributions to the sickness insurance and pension insurance systems. It is methodologically guided by the Ministry of Labour and Social Affairs. Without any doubt, it is the most important social security body in the Czech Republic, as it runs two very important and costly systems of social insurance – pensions and sickness insurance.

61. As a public institution, the General Health Insurance Company can also be mentioned, whereas all the other health insurance companies should be classified as private.

62. As of 1 January 2012, the importance of regional branches of the Labour Office of the Czech Republic (hereinafter RBLO) increased decisively after they became institutions responsible for all non-contributory systems. Currently, they run not only state social support but also all the systems of social assistance. This is due to a radical reform of the organization of social security, the legislation having been adopted in November 2011 and entered into force just some weeks later. No wonder many problems have arisen, which has caused a lot of disappointment among the clients and also the officials of Labour Offices, who fell under tremendous pressure from the public.[6]

6. In more detail on this cf. Koldinská, K. Sociální pomoc. In Koldinská, K., Tröster, P. (eds.) Právo sociálního zabezpečení, C.H. Beck. Praha 2018, pp. 255-256.

63. The Labour Office of the Czech Republic (the central administration) is headed by a director appointed and dismissed by the Minister of Labour and Social Affairs. Her/his appointment is based on the results of a competition, as a rule. This office guides and leads its regional branches, under which local branches work and provide non-contributory benefits. The legal position of the Labour Office of the Czech Republic is defined by Act No. 73/2011 Coll. on the Labour Office of the Czech Republic.

Chapter 2. Position and Competence of the Public Institutions

64. The position and competencies of the public institutions in the field of social security are quite strong as there are only a few fields which may be run by private institutions. These, of course, vary according to the field of social security – there are different public institutions' competencies in different areas of social insurance and also in the area of non-contributory benefits, and the competencies of Labour Offices differ from one subsystem to the other.

§1. Health Insurance

65. State administration of health insurance companies is only exceptional and occurs only in the instances of their origin, termination and control of their activities. However, experience has shown that the state should be provided with more efficient instruments for the implementation of its constitutional responsibility for the assurance of the rights of citizens to reasonable availability of healthcare of adequate quality, scope and price in accordance with the economic possibilities of the health insurance system and the state.

66. While the General Health Insurance Company of the Czech Republic was established directly by an Act (Act of the Czech National Council No. 551/1991 Coll., as amended), the foundation of a sector, branch, enterprise and other health insurance companies (so-called employees' insurance companies) necessitates permission being granted according to general administrative procedural regulations by the Ministry of Health after a previous statement by the Ministry of Finance. Statutory public health insurance is implemented by health insurance companies, which are actually private companies registered in the commercial register, and must meet several conditions in order to be established, as explained below. However, they administer a public system of health insurance and so actually play the role of public institutions; that is why their competencies and functions are explained here and not in the section on private institutions.

67. The self-governing bodies of health insurance companies (boards of directors and supervisory boards) include the representatives of insured persons, insured persons' employers and the state. The representatives of insured persons are always elected by the public administration authorities specified by the law in the case of bodies of the General Health Insurance Company of the Czech Republic, and by the Chamber of Deputies of the Parliament and according to the election rules of the respective employees' insurance company in the case of other health insurance companies.

68. The organizational structure of the General Health Insurance Company of the Czech Republic comprises the central office with its seat in Prague, regional detached agencies for higher self-government territorial units and further territorial offices. The organizational structure of the employees' insurance companies is determined by their statutes as approved by the Ministry of Health.

69. Anyone applying for permission to found an employees' insurance company must evidence primarily professional, financial and organizational qualifications for the operation of an employees' insurance company, the realistic character of envisaged income and expenditure, and assure that the obligation will be met to have at least 100,000 clients within one year of the foundation of the company; further, before the submission of the application the applicant must pay a security of Czech Crown (CZK) 100 million.

70. An employees' insurance company may be terminated by its amalgamation with the General Health Insurance Company of the Czech Republic or by merger or fusion with another employees' insurance company. Permission for the merger or amalgamation of employees' insurance companies will be issued by the Ministry of Health after a prior statement from the Ministry of Finance. In case of rejection of the health insurance plan, financial statement or annual report of an employees' insurance company, the Ministry of Health may also decide on the termination and liquidation of the insurance company.

71. The activities of all health insurance companies are supervised by the Ministry of Health in cooperation with the Ministry of Finance. If checks ascertain serious shortcomings, the ministries can introduce forced administration of the insurance company for a period not exceeding one year. The administrator, who must be an employee of one of the above-mentioned ministries, is authorized to employ further persons for the exercise of forced administration. The administrator and his staff are authorized to familiarize themselves with all facts concerning the respective health insurance company.

§2. Sickness Insurance

72. The administrative authorities authorized to act in the field of sickness insurance include primarily the CSSA (through its DSSA) and the Ministry of Labour and Social Affairs.

73. The DSSA assures the sickness insurance of all insured persons and also fulfils further tasks relating to sickness insurance provided by the law.

74. The Ministry of Defence ensures the payment of sickness benefits to professional soldiers, the Ministry of Interior to the members of the Police of the Czech Republic and of the Fire Rescue Service of the Czech Republic, the Penitentiary Service of the Czech Republic to members of this service and to convicted persons, General Directorate of Customs to members of Customs Administration of the Czech Republic; the payment of these benefits to the members of other armed security services or intelligence agencies is ensured directly by these institutions.

§3. Pension Insurance

75. State administration in the field of pension insurance is exercised by the Ministry of Labour and Social Affairs, the CSSA, the DSSA and the Ministries of Defence, Interior and Justice within the fields of their competence. The CSSA decides in most cases – *see* below in part VIII Pensions.

§4. Employment Policy and Care for the Unemployed

76. The exercise of state administration in order to guarantee the smooth application of state employment policy is managed and controlled by the Ministry of Labour and Social Affairs (in the framework of which the Employment Services Administration is established as a specific department). In particular, it manages the Labour Offices, exercises control activities, administers funds, elaborates predictions of employment development and state-wide concepts and programmes of state employment policy, and solves fundamental labour market problems concerning, for example, the employment of disabled persons and job applicants requiring special care and carries out some further tasks.

77. The administration of the system of employment policy, as such, is ensured by a state institution – the Labour Office of the Czech Republic through its local branches. Their competencies are regulated by Act No. 73/2011 Coll. on the Labour Office of the Czech Republic and also by Act No. 435/2004 Coll. on employment.

78. Certain tasks in the field of employment are also fulfilled by employers (natural and legal persons employing other natural persons in labour law relations) and municipalities. On the basis of a written agreement with the respective RBLO, the employer provides socially useful jobs and generates (analogously with municipalities) publicly beneficial works creating new jobs.

§5. Industrial Accidents and Occupational Diseases

79. The tasks of state administration in this field are assured primarily by the Ministry of Finance. If the respective insurance company (joint-stock companies, the Czech Insurance Company or the Cooperative) suffers material damage through the operation of statutory insurance of the employer's liability for damage due to an industrial accident or an occupational disease, it is entitled to request for a refund of such damage from the state budget. The Ministry of Finance pays proven material damage for the preceding year by, at the latest, 30 June of the current year. By the same date, the above-mentioned insurance companies remit the insurance surplus to the state budget. The Ministry of Finance is also authorized by law to define further details of statutory insurance conditions and insurance rates. This system is being criticized for a long time for two main reasons. Even if the system seems to be a public one, it is run by two private companies, who have a monopoly in this field, and it is not possible to use the services of any other insurance company. At the same time, as the system is fully guaranteed by the State, there is no motivation for employers to improve working conditions or security at the workplace, there is no system of e.g. bonuses or maluses which would influence the amount of contributions obligatorily paid by the employer.

§6. State Social Support

80. State administration of state social support benefits is exercised by offices of state social support, which are the RBLO. The RBLO run the whole system and provide all benefits under state social support. The Ministry of Labour and Social Affairs is authorized by law to perform inspections. The Ministry is also an appeal institution.

§7. Social Assistance

81. Social assistance, similarly to state social support, as a system of non-contributory benefits, is administrated by the RBLO. These offices acquired new competence as of 1 January 2012 in the framework of a reform of the administration of non-contributory benefits. The reason for all non-contributory benefits being entrusted to the Labour Office was for efficiency, better control, and also to combat the misuse of benefits, especially of social assistance benefits.

82. There are, however, still many discrepancies in the new system of administration of social assistance; competencies are not as yet very clear, and the current situation is quite uncertain and chaotic for the clients of the system. Moreover, it seems that the RBLO are not making use of enough social workers, as previously the administration of state social support (which was entrusted to the RBLO as well) did not require any social work with the client. The system of social assistance, as a principle, however, requires social work with the individual client in order to solve each case individually. For this work, however, it seems that there is as yet not enough capacity.

83. Currently, the RBLO have the right to monitor the standard of social services provided and the observance of necessary, particularly, medical and hygienic conditions, and to impose measures remedying any ascertained shortcomings. They decide on the provision of the care allowance – a benefit provided from the system of social services. Moreover, the Labour Offices decide whether and in which form to provide aid in material need benefits, and last but not least, also provide benefits to persons with disabilities.

§8. Public Healthcare

84. Public healthcare in the Czech Republic is codified by Act No. 258/2000 Coll. on public health protection. This Act defines public health as the state of health of the population and its groups and the sum of natural, living and working conditions determining these. Care for public health is based on the responsibility of individuals, families, legal and natural persons in business activities and other subjects. The task of the state is to provide a legislative framework for this responsibility and favourable conditions for local, regional branch and other activities, to provide material support and to maintain a system of professional health service centres concerned with services for public health, its enhancement and protection.

85. Public health protection and enhancement are deemed as the sum of activities and measures intended for the generation and protection of healthy living and working conditions and the prevention of the proliferation of infectious and epidemic diseases, work-related diseases and other significant health disorders. It also includes overseeing the observance of these activities and measures.

86. State administration in the field of public health protection is exercised by public health protection bodies, including:

- the Ministry of Health;
- Regional Hygienic Stations; and
- the Ministry of Defence and the Ministry of Interior.

87. The Ministry of Health manages and assesses the exercise of state administration in public health protection, manages and controls Regional Hygienic Stations and decides on remedies for wrongful decisions, manages inoculations, orders extraordinary measures in case of epidemics, orders protective measures against the displacement of infectious diseases from abroad, assures international cooperation, and it fulfils other tasks provided in the Act on Protection of Public Health.

88. Under the framework of the Ministry of Health, there is the post of Chief Hygienist of the Czech Republic who acts as the representative of the ministry in matters concerning public health protection. The Chief Hygienist of the Czech Republic is appointed and dismissed by the government of the Czech Republic upon the proposal of the Minister of Health.

89. There are fourteen Regional Hygienic Stations in the Czech Republic whose headquarters and administrative areas are specified in the annexe to the aforementioned act. Regional Hygienic Stations are administration bodies incorporating regional offices. Their competence includes, primarily, the issuance of decisions, permits and certificates and the fulfilment of other tasks of state administration in public health protection, including state medical supervision and the fulfilment of other tasks specified in section 82, paragraph 2, of the quoted Act. The content of state medical supervision is defined in section 84 of the Act.

90. The Ministries of Defence and the Interior fulfil the tasks of state administration in public health protection including state medical supervision in armed forces and armed security corps (except for the Penitentiary Service of the Czech Republic). The Ministry of the Interior fulfils the tasks of state administration in public health protection according to the above-mentioned Act, also for the needs of the Administration of International Relations and Information, the Security Intelligence Service and the Fire Rescue Corps of the Czech Republic.

Chapter 3. Private Institutions

91. In the field of social security, non-state and/or public or private law subjects operate in various sectors both in the performance or provision of care and services and in their financing. These activities include primarily:

- healthcare provision in non-state medical institutions;
- employment mediation against payment by private legal or natural persons;
- the provision of social services by non-state subjects (municipalities and districts in the frame of their autonomous areas of activity, non-government organizations of a non-profit character, natural persons); and
- implementation of supplementary pension insurance as a supplementary pension system.

92. The individual types can be characterized as follows.

§1. Non-state Medical Institutions

93. A non-state medical institution may be operated by a natural or legal person authorized under Act No. 272/2011 Coll. on healthcare services. Authorization for the provision of healthcare services is based on a decision on registration issued by the respective regional office according to the place of operation of the institution. The healthcare services provider must be adequately equipped personally, materially and technically for the type and scope of medical care provided and must satisfy requirements imposed upon its operation (in particular, related to hygiene).

94. The healthcare services are provided without direct payment on the basis of public health insurance and the contracts are concluded with health insurance companies, or against direct payment by the person to whom the medical care has been provided, or by a combination of both ways of payment. A non-state institution is obliged to conclude a contract on healthcare provision also with the region competent for the issue of the decision on registration if requested to do so by this body. The goal is to ensure healthcare in the territory under its control in the public interest (*see* below), namely in emergencies.

§2. Private Employment Mediation

95. Apart from the respective state authorities (Labour Offices), a legal or natural person may also mediate employment, if granted permission by the Ministry of Labour and Social Affairs to engage in such activity. While the Labour Offices mediate employment free of charge, the above-mentioned persons may mediate employment against payment even for profit-making purposes. For the purpose of this Act, employment mediation is deemed to mean activity aimed both at searching for a suitable job for a citizen seeking employment and searching for employees on behalf of an employer seeking new manpower. Employment mediation also includes consulting and advisory services.[7]

§3. Non-state Subjects Providing Social Services

96. Social services, especially residential ones, are often provided by municipalities and regions. There is no preference given to NGOs as social services providers are regulated by the Social Services Act, and hence, it does not matter who provides the social services – whether it is an NGO, a for-profit private organization, or a municipality or region. In fact, in the Czech Republic, there still exist some big institutions run by regions, especially for people with disabilities.

97. However, NGOs provide a lot of social services across the whole country. The sector of non-profit provision of social services is already quite developed, even though social services providers still face a lot of organizational and also financial problems. The NGOs are usually established as legal persons in the form of an association or institution (according to the Civil Code), a publicly beneficial company or church legal person.

98. The state grants financial support to such NGOs without any entitlement, however, and always only for one year. This causes financial and also organization uncertainty to the NGOs, their employees and also to their clients. Therefore, NGOs try to find funding from other sources also, such as private donations, projects financed by EU funds, foundations and so on.

§4. Pension Companies

99. Apart from the basic obligatory pension insurance, additional pension insurance as a supplementary pension system was introduced in the Czech Republic in 1994. This system still works, but it is not possible anymore to make a new contract with a pension fund (original pension funds were obliged to transform their capital into transformed funds run by pension companies, according to the Act No. 427/2011 Coll.). As of 2013, it is possible to make a contract with a pension company running supplementary pension savings system. The state supports the supplementary pension savings by state contributions in order to encourage people to join the system (this was very important especially at the beginning, when the system was established and was something completely new for the Czech population), but is not liable for the obligations of pension companies and does not guarantee the individual claims of their beneficiaries. Also, employers' participation in supplementary pension saving system of their employees is permitted to a certain extent. However,

7. On social aspects of the activity of work agencies, *see* Koldinská, K. K problematice sociálního zabezpečení při agenturním zaměstnávání, in Pichrt, J. (edt.) Agenturní zaměstnávání v komplexních souvislostech. C.H. Beck. Praha 2013.

the system does not apply the classical employment (professional) principle based on the relations of pension fund/company – employer – employee. The system applies the civic principle – supplementary pension savings based on the relation of a pension fund and a natural person and represents a system of individual pension savings (third pillar).

100. Pension companies are established, upon authorization provided by the Czech National Bank, if conditions set out in the Act are met. The pension company can invest quite freely, with respect to rules of good administration. The economy of the company is divided from the economy of funds of participants.

Part II. Contribution and Financing

101. The difference between state financing of social benefits and financing through social insurance can be explained, with a certain simplification, as follows: in the state system, the citizens pay taxes which flow to the treasury from which the citizens are paid social security benefits on the basis of the state (Parliament)-approved budget under the conditions provided by the law. This state system was applied in the territory of the Czech Republic until 1992. In the social insurance system, however, the citizen (natural person) insures himself obligatorily for the case that in the future some so-called social event (presumed and closely specified by law) arises; in economic terminology: the individual postpones a part of his 'immediate consumption' for a later period. It is also common that the natural person does not insure himself/herself on his/her own, but he/she is obligatory insured by somebody else (employer, state).

102. Social insurance is based primarily on the principles of mutuality and solidarity. *Mutuality* is understood as assistance granted to individuals who need it from the funds generated by other participants on the basis of ongoing (pay as you go) financing system. *Solidarity* is understood as the solidarity between generations (inter-generation solidarity), i.e., the solidarity of the young with the old (e.g., in case of old-age pensions), the solidarity within one generation (intra-generation solidarity), i.e., the solidarity of the healthy with the sick (health insurance or disability insurance) or the solidarity of the wealthy with the poor (the contributions to the system by the former and the use of its funds by the latter or higher contributions to the system by the former and lower contribution by the latter). Moreover, the system also applies other principles, such as the principle of 'merit' or 'equivalency' (entitlement to the benefit in the amount set out due to the personal merit, i.e., the number of years the beneficiary has worked and the amount of his earnings i.e., the amount of contributions paid by him – typical for pension insurance), or the principle of *equality* (in the meaning of equal rules for benefit entitlement).

103. The social insurance system requires a reliable estimate – on the basis of appropriate mathematical formulas – of costs, the ascertainment of revenue and expenditures, and on their basis the determination of the amount of contributions to be paid by the member of the system (an employee or a self-employed person) or employee's employer (private entrepreneur or state) or, in some cases, the state on behalf of the natural person on the principle of domicile (permanent residence). This process must take into account all relevant circumstances, such as the development of employment, the development of wages, demographic aspects, such as the development of population ageing, the probable development of mortality of insured persons or old-age pensioners and a number of other circumstances.

104. The measures set up by this process also change through the years if the evolvement of these parameters is different from the presumptions. It is impossible, for example, to permit the solution of the future demographic problems at the cost of the present generation; therefore, it is necessary to seek new ways, e.g., analogously with life insurance based on capital principle (first the accumulation of capital and then the payment of benefits). This accumulation of capital reserves, however, should not result in the remittance of the surplus to the state budget. On the contrary, the so-accumulated funds should be concentrated, as economists say, in an autonomous social insurance fund, kept separately from the state budget and administered as a public institution managed by self-governing bodies.

105. In the 1990s, the Czech Government undertook to draft a new codification of pension and sickness insurance financing through the separate account of the state budget. The process of separation of social insurance from the state budget was launched by the payment of insurance contributions as separate payments outside the taxation system and by the establishment on 1 January 1993 of a separate pension insurance account as a part of the financial assets of the state as of 1 January 1996. However, the insurance contributions have remained as state budget revenue from which the costs of both pension and sickness insurance are paid. (These social payments are classified as mandatory state budget expenditure.) Apart from social security insurance contributions, the state budget revenue includes also the derived revenue, i.e., the revenue related to the existence of social security insurance contributions, such as penalties, surcharges to social security insurance and fines. However, it is necessary to admit that in the Czech political and economic environment, this acquisition is not functional – in times of economic conjuncture, the surpluses of the system were used for other purposes, and later (in times of economic crises) the system missed these financial resources, and it was necessary to rescue the shortfall of the pension system from other parts of the state budget. Only the health insurance has not passed through the state budget since its introduction (1 January 1993), and the health insurance contributions are the principal source of revenue of the public health insurance funds of health insurance companies.

106. On the basis of the material of a bill approved by the Government, the intention was to establish by law a Social Insurance Company on 1 January 2002 as a public law institution which should administer both social insurance types. The Social Insurance Company should have to take over all activities of the present insurance carrier – The Czech Social Insurance Administration – except for the assessment service for other social systems or subsystems (state social support, social care, etc.). The Social Insurance Company as a public law subject, in this way, had to become an executive body established by the law to assure the constitutional right of the citizens, managed by self-governing bodies on a tripartite basis, i.e., consisting of the representatives of the insured persons, the employers and the state. In 2018, we still could not enunciate that this concept was definitely rejected

– although the sphere of authority on this field still remains in the hands of the CSSA, the considerations about pension institution separate from the state still occur, especially after the parliamentary elections in October 2017.

107. The second decade of the twenty-first century is dedicated to the 'large reform' of pension systems. The main goals are to:

- ensure a sustainable development of the state pension insurance system established by the Act No. 155/1995 Coll. on the 'pay as you go' principle (so-called first pillar) – the 'retirement age' shall increase, the minimum length of insurance period necessary for entitlement to old-age pension shall extend, measures for reduction of 'early old-age pension' are less favourable, some 'alternative insurance periods' are abolished, etc.;
- empower the 'capital-funding principle' to the level where it would represent the full-value partner of the 'pay as you go' strategy.

108. By Act No. 426/2011 Coll. on pension savings, which came into force on 1 January 2013, there a so-called second pillar was established based on the capital-funding financing model with voluntary membership. The component part of this pillar was so-called 'opt-out conception' – the people who decided for membership in the second pillar had to contribute less to the first pillar (25% of calculation base instead of 28%) – the rest 3% they had to pay to the second pillar and moreover they were obliged to add another 2% to them (so, they paid 5% in addition to the second pillar). The entry to the second pillar was allowed to people younger than 35 years of age. Getting out of the system was not possible. Benefits: life term old-age pension, old-age pension for twenty years, orphan's pension for five years; to withdraw the lump-sum at the end of the saving will not be possible. The administration of the agenda was entrusted to 'pension companies' – legal persons of private law. The state did not contribute to individual accounts of such insured persons. Immediately after the introduction of this system, it was clear that it would not be successful – after one year of existence of this specific form of 'second pillar', it had only 80,000 members. Because of this unattractiveness, the new government decided on the derogation of this system. On 1 January 2016 came into force Act No. 376/2015 Coll. on termination of the pension savings. From this date, it is not allowed to carry on the opt-out procedure, so all the people performing a gainful activity are obliged to pay the premium of up to 28% of their calculation base to the first pillar regardless of the fact that they eventually entered the second pillar in the past. During 2016, the total value of each 'second pillar' pension fund was divided between the participants. The respective shares were paid to them as a lump-sum during the fourth quarter of 2016. Within 2017, the participants were allowed to pay 60% of the lump-sum to social security authority – if they did it, their participation in the second pillar would not impact the amount of their prospective old-age pension from the first pillar. If they did not pay the money back to the social security authority, they must expect that their old-age pension from the first pillar will be lower.

109. Act No. 427/2011 Coll. on complementary pension savings brought a particular reform of the 'third pillar', which was established and had been functional since 1994. This pillar is also based on the capital-funding financing model with voluntary membership but without the 'opt-out' conception. It is fully independent of the first pillar. The members of the complementary saving system have a right to get a state contribution, which is put to credit on their individual accounts conducted by the administrator every month. Getting out of the system is possible anytime. Benefits: old-age pension for a determined period, invalidity pension for a determined period, lump-sum, surrender. The administration of the agenda is also entrusted to 'pension companies'. It is common that the contributions to the saving are paid by the employer in favour of his employee. Paying off the contributions means tax allowance for the contributor. In contrast to the 'second pillar', the 'third pillar' is very popular – in 2018, it had approx. 5 million participants. In connection with the above-mentioned Act No. 376/2015 Coll. on the termination of pension savings, there are some new provisions for further consolidation of attraction of the 'third pillar'.

110. Broadly, the term social insurance also covers, apart from sickness and pension insurance, health insurance, unemployment insurance and accident insurance. With the exception of the last one, the systems of all these insurance types were established in the Czech Republic and have been continuously developed since the end of the twentieth century and the beginning of the twenty-first century. *Health* insurance is obligatory for all persons with a permanent residence in the territory of the Czech Republic, as well as the persons with no permanent residence in the territory of the Czech Republic but employed by an employer with the registered place of business in the territory of the Czech Republic. Participation in *pension* insurance is obligatory for natural persons (performing a gainful activity in the territory of the Czech Republic) specified in the Act, in the first place for the employees in an employment relationship and the persons in analogous labour relations, the persons in service relationship and other legal relations and self-employed persons; insured are also people within the so-called alternative insurance periods (people taking care of children younger than 4 years or some other dependent persons, registered applicants for a job, etc.). The personal scope of application in the field of *sickness* insurance is analogous except for self-employed persons whose sickness insurance is voluntary; in sickness insurance, there are no 'alternative insurance periods'.

Chapter 1. Contribution Regulation for Employees

§1. Field of Application

I. Territorial Field of Application

111. Social security and state employment policy contributions, as well as the public health insurance contributions form the principal sources of revenue intended for the financing of these fields in the Czech Republic.

112. The scope of territorial application of the contributions to social insurance and state employment policy, as well as the scope of territorial application of the contributions to public health insurance are determined by the territorial applicability of the respective Acts. These Acts, i.e., Act No. 589/1992 Coll. on social security contributions and the contribution to state employment policy, Act No. 48/1997 Coll. on public health insurance and the amendments and supplements of some other Acts (Part Two) and Act No. 592/1992 Coll. on general health insurance, all as amended, are applicable in the *whole territory of the Czech Republic*. The sickness insurance contributions together with pension insurance contributions form social security insurance contributions paid jointly with the contribution to the state employment policy.

113. The territorial aspect expresses itself in the field of *health insurance* in the necessity to have permanent residence in the territory of the Czech Republic or to be employed by an employer with the registered place of business in the territory of the Czech Republic.

114. The territorial aspect expresses itself in the field of *pension and sickness insurance* in the necessity to perform working activity in the territory of the Czech Republic or (when the working activity is performed abroad) to have an employer with the registered place of business in the territory of the Czech Republic – one of these conditions must be fulfilled by employees whose participation on insurance is obligatory. For people whose participation on pension insurance is voluntary (they want to be insured even if they do not fulfil the conditions of obligatory participation), the territorial aspect is not taken into account. The territorial aspect is also not taken into account by so-called foreign employees whose participation in Czech sickness insurance is voluntary and is indeed conditioned by their voluntary participation in pension insurance.

II. Personal Field of Application

115. The scope of persons paying social security and state employment policy contributions includes:

– employers (legal or natural persons);

- employees and people performing activities on the basis of similar legal relationships such as civil servants, members of cooperatives, judges, deputies and senators, president, members of the Government, members of municipal and regional boards and others;
- self-employed persons, if participating in pension or sickness insurance; and
- persons participating voluntarily in pension insurance during the period of this participation.

116. Social insurance or state employment policy contributions are not paid by pensioners (beneficiaries of pension insurance), the unemployed and other specific groups of persons who do not perform any gainful activity.

117. Contributions to *public health insurance* are paid by the insured persons, the employers and the state through the state budget for the enumerated groups of persons. The state pays the contributions for dependent children, pensioners, women on maternity and parenthood leave, job applicants (i.e., the unemployed), persons performing military service, persons in custody or serving the penalty of imprisonment, etc.

118. In the Public Health Insurance Act, the scope of insured persons includes the employees in employment relationship, if participating in health insurance, as well as the persons considered as employees (i.e., an analogous group of natural persons as specified above in case of social security insurance); their number also includes self-employed persons and other persons with permanent residence in the territory of the Czech Republic (residents).

§2. Calculation of Contributions

I. Calculation Base

119. The employee's calculation base is the scope of her/his income accurately defined by the Act. The regulation is practically identical for social security insurance and public health insurance. The calculation base of employees is the sum of their incomes which are subject to income tax (and are not free of tax) and were accounted by their employer in relation to the performance of their employment connected with participation on sickness insurance. The term 'accounted income' means for this purpose performance, which was in pecuniary or non-pecuniary form or in the form of advantage provided to an employee by his employer or given in favour of him or put to his credit or, in other forms of performance, realized by an employer on behalf of his employee.

120. Regardless of the previous paragraph, these listed below are *not included* in the employee's calculation base:

- compensation of damages;
- severance money or payoff;

- loyalty bonuses of mineworkers;
- benefit, which was given to the beneficiary of old-age pension or of third-degree invalidity pension after a lapse of one year from the day of termination of his employment;
- lump-sum pecuniary social support provided to an employee by his employer to bridge over extremely difficult situations caused by a natural disaster, fire, ecological or industrial accident or other extremely serious events, and some others.

121. Moreover, the General Health Insurance Act provides certain deviations. Thus, for instance, the employee's contribution is based on the minimum calculation base which is the minimum wage (amounting to CZK 12,200 as of 1 January 2018). Analogously, if the employee's calculation base is lower than the minimum calculation base, the employee is obliged to pay the appropriate health insurance company, through his employer, the contribution amounting to 13.5% of the difference of these calculation bases. If the employee is a person for whom the insurance has also been paid by the state, her/his calculation base is the amount exceeding the amount of the calculation base of the person for whom the insurance is paid by the state (with effect from 1 January 2018, this amount has been CZK 7,177).

122. From 2008, the above-stated Acts contain a provision which regulates the so-called *maximum calculation base*. From its establishment, this amount of money used to be common for 'social insurance' and 'health insurance'. However, from 2012, this amount was not the same and represented:

- 72-multiple of state average wages per calendar year for the purposes of health insurance (CZK 1,809,864 – valid for 2012); from 2013 the *maximum calculation base* for the premium on health insurance was definitely abolished;
- 48-multiple of state average wages per calendar year for the purposes of sickness and pension insurance (CZK 1,355,136 – valid for 2017, CZK 1,438,992 – valid for 2018).

123. People who earn more money per year than the amount of 'maximum calculation base' do not pay contributions from the amount of money surpassing the amount of 'maximum calculation base'.

II. Contribution Amount

124. The amount of contributions is determined as a percentage of the calculation base for the decisive period. Unless provided differently, the decisive period for calculation base determination is the calendar month for which the contribution is paid.

125. The percentage rates of *social security and state employment policy* contributions are different for individual contributor types and amount to:

- 25% for employers, of which 2.3% fall to sickness insurance, 21.5% to pension insurance and 1.2% to state employment policy;
- 6.5% for employees which fall to pension insurance (until 2015 employees who were a party to the pension savings according to Act No. 426/2011 Coll. on pension savings paid 3.5% – the other 3% were transferred to their individual accounts within the respective fund of pension savings.

126. The amount of contribution to health insurance is 13.5% of the calculation base for the decisive period. One-third (i.e., 4.5%) of this contribution is paid by the employee, two-thirds (9%) by the employer.

127. The fundamental rule for the employers is that they pay the social security insurance with the contribution to state employment policy, as well as the health insurance contributions not only 'for themselves' but also for their employees. Exceptions to this rule are mentioned below.

§3. Reductions and Exemptions

128. There are no reductions applicable to social security and state employment policy contributions or public health insurance contributions in the Czech Republic.

129. From the participation in health insurance are exempted:

- who, in the territory of the Czech Republic, perform an 'illegal work' in the sense of Act No. 435/2004 Coll. on employment;
- who do not have permanent residence in the territory of the Czech Republic and perform a working activity for an employer who enjoys diplomatic advantages or immunities or who does not have a registered place of business in the territory of the Czech Republic;
- who are on a long-term stay (uninterrupted stay exceeding six months) abroad, where they are subject to health insurance, and who have suspended their health insurance with their health insurance company in Czech Republic for that period; during this period of time, such person does not have a right on free of charge healthcare in the Czech Republic.

130. The insured person is exempted from the obligation to pay health insurance contributions if her/his contributions are paid by the state. The state pays health insurance contributions through the state budget for dependent children, pensioners, family allowance beneficiaries, women on maternity leave and parenthood leave, job applicants (i.e., the unemployed), social care beneficiaries, mostly or completely incapacitated persons or persons taking care of such persons, persons in custody or serving the penalty of imprisonment, etc. If these persons have some income from employment or self-employment, the insurance contributions are paid jointly by the state and by these persons.

§4. CONTRIBUTION SURCHARGE

131. Social security contribution surcharge is imposed by the appropriate DSSA upon the employer if, according to a legally effective decision of the appropriate state supervisory body, his plant does not satisfy the requirements of the occupational safety and health protection regulations or medical or hygienic regulations or if the required equipment for the employees' life and health protection does not operate. The imposed surcharge may amount to as much as 5% of the sum of calculation bases of all his employees in the individual months to which the surcharge applies.

132. Analogous sanctions, such as penalties, fines and surcharges to insurance contributions, are applied also in the field of *health insurance*.

133. Health insurance contribution surcharge may be imposed by the appropriate health insurance company upon the employer in whose enterprise industrial accidents and occupational diseases due to the same reasons recurred in the past year, as a result of which the healthcare costs also grew accordingly. Such surcharge may attain 5% of the quota of insurance contributions of all employees paid by him.

§5. CONTRIBUTIONS PAID BY BENEFICIARIES

134. If the beneficiary of 'old-age pension' or 'third-stage invalidity pension' re-enters an employment relationship or any other legal relation establishing his participation in sickness insurance, his employer is obliged to pay the appropriate social insurance and state employment policy contributions, as well as public health insurance contributions 'for himself' and for this employee.

135. This applies regardless of the fact that the beneficiaries of these pensions are entitled to sickness benefits during the same incapacity to work only for seventy calendar days and in more cases of incapacity to work amounting to only seventy calendar days in one calendar year.

136. However, from 2010 the paying of social insurance contributions has a positive influence on the amount of the admitted pension. If the pensioner, during the enjoying of his pension, has completed at least 360 days of 'period of insurance', he acquires the right to increase his pension of 0.4% of the computational base. Before 2010, the paying of social insurance contributions did not have any positive influence on the amount of the admitted pension – it was paid only as an aspect of solidarity in the pension system.

§6. ADMINISTRATION

137. The employers – legal or natural persons employing other natural persons – fulfil the prescribed obligations concerning the calculation and payment of social insurance and state employment policy contributions, as well as the calculation and payment of public health insurance contributions.

138. For the purpose of *sickness insurance* and *pension insurance* (together called as 'social insurance' in a narrower sense), the 'Act on sickness insurance' and 'Act No. 582/1991 Coll. on social security organization and application' give a very extensive and detailed definition (both acts are the same in substance) in which the subject (natural or legal person or organizational unit of the state) is considered an employer of one of the various categories of employees. In previous times, the employers were divided into two groups ('organizations' with more than twenty-five employees and 'small organizations' with less than twenty-six employees) with a different range of duties – this diversification was abolished in 2009; from this year, all employers have the same duties in social insurance.

139. Because of the fact that sickness insurance and pension insurance are closely linked (the participation of employees on pension insurance is fully conditioned by participation on sickness insurance, the calculation base for contribution is identical), the employers often fulfil their tasks in both these systems (and also state employment policy) in common. In particular, employers are obliged to:

- register themselves and the employees to DSSA and 'apply' them for the insurance;
- gather the basis for determination of the amount of contributions (wages, calculation bases) and to keep a record of them;
- calculate the amount of the contribution and pay theirs and the employee's part of the contribution on behalf of employees to the DSSA at the prescribed time; and
- cooperate with the respective DSSA, if necessary.

140. By failure to perform their duties, they are obliged to sustain fines, penalties or other sanctions.

141. Very similar tasks and duties fulfil the employers also in the field of *health insurance*. Within this agenda, they cooperate with health insurance companies.

142. Statutory insurance contributions to public health insurance are administered by the respective health insurance companies as public law subjects. The health insurance companies are financial institutions 'sui generis'. They generate their own accounting and information system which they administer. These information systems must be compatible with the state statistical records. The register of all insured persons is kept by the General Health Insurance Company of Czech Republic which notifies the Ministry of Finance every month of the changes in the number of insured persons for whom the state pays insurance contributions.

143. The self-governing bodies of health insurance companies (boards of directors, supervisory boards) consist of the representatives of insured persons, employers and the state. The representatives of insured persons are always elected; in the case of the bodies of the General Health Insurance Company of the Czech Republic, they are elected by the Chamber of Deputies of the Parliament, in the case of the bodies of the so-called employees' insurance companies, they are elected according to the election rules of the respective insurance company. The representatives of employers of insured persons in the Board of Directors and in the Supervisory Board of the General Health Insurance Company of Czech Republic are appointed and recalled by organizations of employers and, in case of employers' insurance companies, they are appointed according to relevant Rules of Election. The representative of the state in the Board of Directors of the General Health Insurance Company of Czech Republic is appointed and recalled by the Government of the Czech Republic and in its Supervisory Board by the Ministry of Finance, Ministry of Labour and Social Affairs and Ministry of Health – one representative for each ministry. In the case of employers' insurance companies, the representative of the state in both relevant bodies is appointed and recalled by the Ministry of Health.

Chapter 2. Contributions for Public Sector Workers

144. As mentioned above, the social security and state employment policy contributions, as well as public health insurance contributions are paid, apart from employees in employment relationship (in both private and public sector), also by the persons exercising public functions enumerated in the Act as their employment; their number includes primarily judges, deputies and senators of the Parliament of Czech Republic, members of municipal and regional boards, members of the Government, the President, Vice-President and members of the Supreme Audit Office, members of the Advisory Board for Radio and TV Broadcasting, the Chairman of the Office for Energetic Regulation, the members of Council of Institute for Study of Totalitarian Regime, the Financial Arbitrator and the Deputy Financial Arbitrator, the Ombudsman and the Deputy Ombudsman. From 2015, the biggest group of 'Public Sector Workers' consists of persons whose gainful activity is subject to Act No. 234/2014 Coll. on civil service.

145. The status of all these groups of 'Public Sector Workers' in the field of 'social insurance' and 'health insurance' is equal to other groups of employees. Their employers are also obliged to fulfil the same tasks and duties.

Chapter 3. Contributions for the Self-Employed

§1. Field of Application

I. Territorial Field of Application

146. Both the Act on social security insurance and the contribution to state employment policy and the Act on general health insurance apply to the whole territory of the Czech Republic which assumes the execution of self-employment activities in the territory of the whole state.

147. The territorial aspect expresses itself in the field of:

- *health* insurance in the necessity to have a permanent residence in the territory of the Czech Republic;
- *pension and sickness insurance* in the necessity to perform self-employment in the territory of the Czech Republic or (when the working activity is performed abroad) to perform it on the basis of licence arising from the Czech legal order. If one of these conditions is fulfilled, the participation of self-employed persons on pension insurance is obligatory; the participation on sickness insurance is voluntary. In both cases, the territorial aspect is taken into account.

II. Personal Field of Application

148. The number of insured persons includes every self-employed person, i.e., every person performing activities forming the source of her/his income on the basis of specific regulations. Their number includes, primarily, the persons operating a trade according to the Trades Act or carry on business in agriculture, the persons operating on the basis of specific regulations (attorneys-at-law, notaries, auditors, tax advisers, judicial experts, interpreters, etc.). Their number also includes the partners in public commercial partnerships and general partners in limited partnerships. Also, cooperating persons and the persons performing art or other creative activities on the basis of copyright regulations are deemed to be self-employed persons.

149. Self-employed persons are obliged to pay contributions to *pension insurance* and the state employment policy if they participate in pension insurance under the pension insurance regulations, as well as advance payments to these contributions under statutory conditions. In some cases (if self-employment is performed beside, e.g., the regular employment or beside studying or simultaneously with enjoying of some pension – so-called adjoining self-employment), the participation on pension insurance and paying contributions is not obligatory if the incomes (tax base) of such self-employment do not reach the amount of 2.4-multiple of the state average wages per year.

150. Self-employed persons are obliged to pay *sickness insurance* contributions or advance payments to these contributions if they participate in sickness insurance, i.e., if they have joined it, as this insurance is voluntary for them.

151. Self-employed persons pay contributions to pension insurance, sickness insurance and the state employment policy to the account of the respective DSSA. The venue is governed by the permanent address of the self-employed person; if the self-employed person has no permanent address in the territory of the Czech Republic, the venue is governed by the place of performance of her/his activities.

152. Every self-employed person is obliged to pay *health* insurance contributions. These contributions are paid to the respective health insurance company by which the self-employed person is insured.

§2. Basis for Calculation of Contributions

153. The calculation base for the amount of social insurance contributions is the amount determined by the self-employed person himself/herself. Its minimum in 2018 was 50% of her/his tax base (the difference between income and costs expended on the achievement, assurance and maintenance of this income). However, the statutory minimum amount of the annual calculation base is CZK 89,940 (12-multiple of one-fourth state average wages) – this minimal amount will be used in the case that the real tax base of self-employed persons does not reach this amount. The maximum amount of the annual calculation base is CZK 1,438,992 (48-multiple of state average wages). The decisive period for calculation base determination of self-employed persons is the calendar year.

154. By persons performing so-called adjoining self-employment in 2018, the minimum amount of the annual calculation base was CZK 35,976 (12-multiple of one-tenth state average wages). The decisive amount of incomes (tax base) which establishes to such person a duty to participate in pension insurance is CZK 71,950 (2.4-multiple of state average wages).

155. If the self-employed person decides for voluntary participation on sickness insurance, she/he is obliged to pay the respective contribution for this purpose. Such person is entitled to determine the monthly calculation base by herself/himself but the amount shall not be lower than CZK 5,000, and at the same time it shall not be higher than the average monthly calculation base for pension insurance contribution used in the last calendar year. In case of *health insurance*, the calculation base amounts to 50% of the income from the business and other activities of self-employed persons after the deduction of expenses required for its achievement, assurance and maintenance. However, the statutory minimum amount of the annual calculation base for 2018 was CZK 179,880 (12-multiple of one-half state average wages) – this minimal amount will be used in the case that the real tax base of self-employed person does not reach this amount; the Act regulates some exceptions from this general rule. The decisive period is the calendar year for which the contributions are paid. Self-employed persons pay the contributions in the form of monthly advance payments and as an annual settlement.

§3. Amount of Contribution

156. The amount of contributions is determined as a percentage of the calculation base ascertained for the decisive period. The contribution rate is 29.2% for the pension insurance and the state employment policy, of which 28% contribute to pension insurance, 1.2% to the state employment policy. A self-employed person who decides for voluntary participation in sickness insurance pays 2.3% of the calculation base.

157. The rate of health insurance is 13.5% of the calculation base.

§4. Administration

158. The contributions to social security and state employment policy are administered by the respective DSSA which, in particular, checks whether the contributions are paid 'properly and in due time'. If the contribution has not been paid within the due period or if a lower than due amount has been paid, the Administration imposes a penalty on the payee. The penalty is not imposed for the period in which the self-employed person does not perform gainful activities. The respective DSSA may permit the payment of owed contributions and penalties by instalments. It may also fine the payee for the failure to comply with or the breach of other obligations provided by the law with a fine amounting to CZK 50,000 for every failure or breach of the respective obligation.

159. The administration of contributions to health insurance, including the monitoring of their payment, is performed by the health insurance companies themselves, which may also impose a penalty on a self-employed person if the contributions or advance payments thereto have not been made in due time or have been paid in a lower amount. The self-employed person may also be fined for the failure to comply with the notification duty.

Chapter 4. Other Contributions

160. In the field of health insurance, this chapter may include some further revenue of funds of the respective health insurance companies outside of insurance contributions. This includes, for example, the revenue from contractual health insurance for insured persons to cover healthcare exceeding the framework of paid healthcare or for persons not subject to statutory insurance. It includes compensation for damages paid by third parties for healthcare costs due to their culpable unlawful action, and it also includes surcharges to insurance contributions and penalties, interest on bank accounts, financial gifts, income from the sale of securities, and so on.

161. Another similar specific payment within health insurance is the so-called regulatory fees. These were introduced into the Czech healthcare system in 2007 in the face of great resistance on the part of left-wing parties. The purpose of these fees was to discourage patients from making pointless visits to physicians and, in general, from the overuse of the healthcare system, where not necessary. In fact, some people used the physician as a social contact with society rather than help with a health problem. The original fees were: CZK 30 (about Euro (EUR) 1.20) for a visit by a doctor, CZK 90 (about EUR 3.5) for a visit by an emergency ambulance, and CZK 100 (about EUR 4) for a day in the hospital. The regulation fee in the hospital was abolished by the decision of the Constitutional Court,[8] the general regulation fee by an amendment to Act No. 48/1997 Coll. on health insurance. The only regulation fee still left is the fee for emergency healthcare (CZK 90). There are limits also to this fee in order to not place an unbearable burden on very ill or socially weak people (section 16a of the Act No. 48/1997 Coll.).

8. Judgment of the Constitutional Court No. Pl. ÚS 36/11 from 20 June 2013.

Chapter 5. Government Funding

162. In the field of social security, the expenses of sickness and pension insurance are paid from the state budget. At the same time, all the contributions to these systems are an income of the state budget (*see* above). Therefore, the social insurance contributions also form a part of the state budget revenue complete with derived items (penalties, surcharges and fines). The pension insurance contributions form an autonomous item of the state budget with a separate account. These funds should be primarily used for an increase in pension benefits and to cover a negative account balance.

163. Thus the sources of social insurance funding in the Czech Republic consist exclusively of budget revenue and expenditure.

Part III. Healthcare

164. A specific feature of the Czech social security system is the separation of health insurance from sickness (or social) insurance, both in respect of its codification, organization and implementation and its financing and administration, as already explained above.

165. The healthcare system underwent a massive reform, which entered into force as of 1 April 2012. The reform was expected for a long time, as the healthcare system is very expensive and not as effective as it could be. Some main healthcare insurance acts were decisively amended, and some new acts regulating the provision of healthcare were adopted.

166. The first amendment through Act No. 369/2011 Coll., amending Act No. 48/1997 Coll., the Public Health Insurance Act, features terminological and similar changes necessary to ensure that the Act is in line with the draft bill on healthcare services. Section 13(2) defines reimbursed services; sections 18 et seq. define the terms and conditions for the provision thereof; while section 32(6) mitigates the ban on granting bonuses and discounts in pharmacies. New Schedules 1–3 apply to medical and therapeutic services, pharmaceuticals and healthcare means and devices.

167. The Healthcare Services Act (Act No. 372/2011 Coll.) is applicable to and governs the basic terms and conditions for the provision of healthcare services. The Act defines the position of providers of healthcare services and the state and the rights and obligations of patients; it also introduces new terminology. The Act distinguishes between healthcare and healthcare services; healthcare facilities themselves do not enjoy a legal personality as per the new definition. Instead, the providers of healthcare services are the bearers of the legal personality. There are rules applicable to how to file and deal with complaints against procedures applied in providing healthcare services. Re-registration is required for both the existing private and state healthcare facilities.

168. Act No. 373/2011 Coll. on specific healthcare services and Act No. 374/2011 Coll. on healthcare rescue and emergency services provide some independent rules, which apply both to so-called specific healthcare services (such as assisted reproduction, sterilization, sex reassignment, etc.), and the terms and conditions for the provision of healthcare rescue and emergency services to persons suffering from a major health disease or to persons in direct threat of death.

Chapter 1. Field of Application

§1. Territorial Field of Application

169. The subjective right to healthcare in the territory of the Czech Republic is declared in Article 31 of the Charter of Fundamental Rights and Freedoms promulgated as a component part of the constitutional system of the Czech Republic by the resolution of the Presidium of the Czech National Council (the legislative body of the Czech Republic) No. 2/1993 Coll. Under this article, 'everyone has the right to health protection'. Further, this article provides that on the basis of public insurance citizens are entitled to free (i.e., without direct payment) healthcare and health aids under the conditions provided by the law. This distinction was confirmed by the Constitutional Court, which ruled that 'the holder of the constitutional right to free public health care is only a citizen of the Czech Republic, while the holder of the right to health protection is any person'.[9]

170. Health insurance companies are used to cover the costs of healthcare provided in the territory of the Czech Republic. The companies are also used to refund clients the amount they have expended on necessary and urgent treatment, the need for which has arisen during their stay abroad, up to the amount provided for such care in the territory of the Czech Republic. The EU coordination Regulations Nos 883/2004 and 987/2009 are applied by the health insurance companies as well, whereas the Health Insurance Bureau (which replaced the Centre of International Reimbursements as of 1 January 2016) works as a liaison body for the purposes of coordination of sickness benefits provided in kind.

171. Healthcare is provided by the medical institutions of the state, municipalities, natural and legal persons (i.e., state or non-state medical institutions), in accordance with state-of-the-art medical science available and within the territory of the Czech Republic.

§2. Personal Field of Application

172. Health insurance covers all persons with permanent residence in the territory of the Czech Republic from birth to death, and persons with no permanent residence in the territory of the Czech Republic if they are employed by an employer with a registered place of business in the territory of the Czech Republic from the day of the start of their employment until its termination. This is called the principle of universality of personal application of health insurance, which means that it is a system of generally valid insurance, available to all persons specified in the act to whom healthcare within the scope defined by the act is granted, and its costs are covered on the basis of uniform codification.

9. Judgment of the Constitutional Court No. Pl. ÚS 2/15 from 2 May 2017

173. Excluded from this are persons with no permanent residence in the Czech Republic working there for an employer with diplomatic immunity, or in a labour law relation concluded on the basis of foreign regulations, or for an employer who does not have a registered address in the territory of the Czech Republic, or for persons staying abroad on a long-term basis (longer than six months) and not paying insurance contributions during that period.

Chapter 2. Benefits

174. According to uniform codification, the funds of obligatory health insurance are used to cover the costs of healthcare provided to entitled persons (insured persons) with the purpose of maintaining or improving their state of health. The scope of healthcare thus covered, and the conditions of its provision and funding are regulated by the Act on Public Health Insurance which imposes on health insurance companies *expressis verbis* the duty to ensure the provision of healthcare for their clients through medical institutions with which they have concluded contracts on healthcare provision and payment.

§1. Care Provided

175. Health insurance covers healthcare granted to an insured person with the purpose of maintaining or improving her/his state of health. With regard to economic possibilities, statutory health insurance cannot cover all medical operations (such as cosmetic operations intended for reasons other than therapeutic purposes, massages if not indicated as a component part of rehabilitation care, acupuncture, or operations performed abroad beyond the framework of necessary and urgent treatment connected with operations performed in the Czech Republic, etc.). However, in such cases, citizens may use supplementary forms of facultative (voluntary) contractual insurance or supplementary insurance. In contrast to this private law contractual relation, statutory health insurance is obligatory insurance of a public law nature.

176. There has been an attempt to enable patients to pay in cash for healthcare services provided above the standard level (which is in reality done by many medical institutions). The amendment of the Health Care Insurance Act was, however, abolished by the Constitutional Court, as the definition of what is above standard was put in Ministerial Order and not in the law.[10]

177. Healthcare granted in the framework of public health insurance includes:

- ambulatory and institutional medical care including diagnostics, rehabilitation, care of chronically sick persons and healthcare for donors of tissues or organs in connection with their delivery;
- first-aid emergency and rescue service;
- preventative care;
- dispensary care;
- delivery of tissues or organs destined for transplantations and necessary treatment of these (preservation, storing, preparation and examination);
- provision of therapeutic preparations, means of medical technology and stomatological products;

10. Judgment of the Constitutional Court No. Pl. ÚS 36/11 from 10 July 2013

- special medical alimentary;
- spa treatment and care in specialized children's institutions and sanatoria;
- preventative care;
- transportation of the sick and compensation for travelling expenses;
- transportation of living donors to the place of delivery and back to the place of medical care in connection with the delivery along with compensation for transportation expenses;
- transportation of dead donors to the place of delivery and back;
- transportation of delivered tissues and organs;
- medical assessments; and
- post-mortem examinations including transportation.

178. Health insurance also covers healthcare in connection with the pregnancy and birth of children that requires the identity of the mother and the children to be kept secret in connection with the birth. Health insurance does not cover healthcare services provided during a home birth. As there is currently a tendency of some women to give birth at home, the legislation has been attacked by the Constitutional Court and also by the European Court of Human Rights (ECHR). The latter Court issued a judgment of Grand Chamber in *Dubska, Krejzova.*[11] The ECHR had not found a violation of the Article 8 of the European Convention on Human Rights and Fundamental Freedoms as the Czech legislation was not found disproportionate. The Court pointed out that the Czech Government has taken some initiatives with a view to improving the situation of mothers-to-be in hospital care, notably by establishing a new governmental expert committee on the issue of obstetrics, midwifery and related women's rights. The Court invited the Czech authorities to make further progress by keeping the relevant legal provisions under constant review, making sure that they reflect medical and scientific developments whilst fully respecting women's' rights in the field of reproductive rights. Ensuring adequate conditions for both patients and medical staff in maternity hospitals across the Czech Republic was one way of achieving this progress. The Court, therefore, concluded that the interference with the applicants' right to a private life had not been disproportionate and held that there had been no violation of Article 8 of the Convention.[12]

§2. Amount of Benefit

179. As healthcare in the Czech Republic is provided only in kind, it is not possible to define the amount of benefit. It can be said, however, that healthcare must always be provided at such a level that protects in the best way the health condition of the patient and corresponds to modern medical knowledge. There might be some types of health treatment which are considered as 'over-standard', where such care is not normally covered by health insurance and must be paid by the patient from

---

11. Judgment of Grand Chamber of the ECHR in *Dubská, Krejzová vs. Czech Republic* from 15.11.2016 application Nos 28859/11, 28473/12.
12. *See* press release to the Judgment in *Dubská Krejzová.*

their own financial sources (like, for example, plastic surgery, giving birth only under the care of the chief doctor, etc.). There has been an attempt to legislate the so-called over-standard, the Constitutional Court, however, abolished such legislation, as the 'over-standard' was not defined by the law, but only by an ordinance of the Ministry of Health.[13]

180. Every natural person must be insured with one of the health insurance companies (the principle of plurality of insurance institutions), which she/he selects himself/herself (section 11, paragraph 1/a of Act No. 48/1997 Coll.). The selection of health insurance company, therefore, is based on the free choice principle. The principle of free choice applies also to the selection of the transportation service, which is in a contractual relationship with the respective health insurance company.

181. Healthcare is provided to insured persons in the form of ambulatory or institutional care (section 18, paragraph 2 of the Public Health Insurance Act). It is a benefit provided in kind, the scope of which is determined by the character and the type of healthcare provided. The fundamental healthcare in ambulatory medical institutions is provided by medical practitioners, children's and youth's medical practitioners, dental practitioners and gynaecologists with whom they have registered. The attending medical practitioner is obliged to instruct adequately the patient or the members of her/his family on the character of her/his ailment and the necessary medical operations. Examination and therapeutic operations are carried out with the patient's consent or where such consent can be presumed. In the case of refusal, the attending physician requests the patient's written declaration thereof. If the immediate performance of the operation is essential to save the life or health of a child, the attending physician is authorized to decide, even where the child's parent refuses to give consent. The patient may be provided with health services only with own informed consent (sections 28 and 34–40 of Act No. 372/2011 Coll.). Any healthcare provider must have evidence of healthcare services provided to patients with their consent. If healthcare services (especially hospitalization) are provided to the patient without her/his consent, the law strictly requires that legal conditions are met (sections 38–39 of Act No. 372/2011 Coll.). The hospital is obliged to report to the competent court about details of providing such healthcare services. The court immediately decides whether hospitalization is necessary and all conditions are met.

182. If an insured person has been granted healthcare in a medical institution with which the respective health insurance company has concluded a contract, the insured person is entitled to healthcare without direct payment (within the scope and under the conditions provided by the law). Contractual medical institutions may not request from the insured person any cash payments for the healthcare provided or in relation thereto.

183. If the patient is not provided with the requisite medicines, therapeutic and orthopaedic aids or other means of medical technology directly, during the provision of healthcare, she/he will receive them upon prescription in a pharmacy or any

---

13. *See* Judgment of the Constitutional Court No. Pl. ÚS 36/11 from 20 Jun. 2013.

other institution established for this purpose. The General Health Insurance Company of the Czech Republic, as well as other health insurance companies established under Act No. 280/1992 Coll. make contracts on healthcare provisions with pharmacies. Also, the aids, replacements and apparatuses used for therapy (including their servicing) are provided and paid for on a contractual basis.

184. The respective health insurance company is entitled to compensation for damages from third parties if it has expended costs on healthcare provided as a result of their culpable unlawful action affecting the person participating in health insurance.

§3. Determining Rates of Fees and Prices

185. The health insurance company, with which the person is insured, is obliged to cover the costs of the healthcare granted to the insured person within the scope and under the conditions provided by the Public Health Insurance Act to the respective medical institution on the basis of a contract concluded with it (section 17 of the quoted act). Although the contract is concluded between the insurance company and the respective medical institution (and is, therefore, a bilateral legal act), the legal relations arising from it are of the character of trilateral relations, between the insured person, the respective medical institution and the respective health insurance company. Such contracts are concluded for the types of healthcare as the respective medical institution is authorized to provide. In the case of a non-state medical institution, the type and scope of healthcare provided arise from the decision on its registration issued by the respective authority (as a rule, regional offices according to the place of operation of the non-state institution). In the case of a state medical institution, the scope of healthcare provided arises from the foundation charter of the institution.

186. The contracted medical institutions (of both state and non-state types) invoice the insurance companies for the healthcare granted according to prices agreed between the representatives of the health insurance companies and the representatives of the healthcare providers. The state does not interfere with the prices determined by these negotiations. However, should these negotiations not reach an agreement within the stipulated period or should the concluded agreement on the price of the healthcare be at variance with legal regulations or the public interest, the respective prices agreed for the preceding period remain in force. In such cases, the amount of the payments and regulation limitations are determined by an ordinance of the Ministry of Health, which changes each year.

187. Medical institutions providing ambulatory or institutional care (institutional care means the care in hospitals and specialized medical in institutions) conclude contracts on healthcare provision with health insurance companies. These contracts must comply with framework contracts under an ordinance of the Ministry of Health.

188. The manner of reimbursement is agreed by the respective medical institution with the respective health insurance company. In 1997, the Public Health Insurance Act broke with the until-then exclusive means of healthcare reimbursement on the basis of point valuation of medical operations and also enabled reimbursement on the basis of lump-sum compensation for services provided. Lump-sum compensation is deemed to mean payments based on the number of insured persons (capitation fee) registered in ambulatory care and an aggregate rate per bed and day or diagnosis in institutional care.

189. As of 2007, the so-called regulatory fees were introduced into the health insurance system. Their purpose was to discourage patients from unnecessary overuse of healthcare, which proved to be very expensive. As was already explained, two of the three regulatory fees were abolished, and only a fee for emergency healthcare service has been kept. The fee is regulated in section 16a and 16b of Act No. 48/1997 Coll., where some limits are also set out for the fees paid per year which are further reduced to certain groups of persons (whereas some other groups, for example, the poor and socially excluded, are exempted from the obligation to pay these fees) in order not to cause social or economic damage to people who cannot afford too high payments during a year.

§4. Budget Limitation

190. Not applicable.

Chapter 3. Conditions

191. Healthcare is provided to people under the condition that they are insured and that their healthcare provider has an agreement with their health insurance company.

192. Basic healthcare to save lives is also provided where the above-mentioned conditions are met. In such cases, healthcare is paid by the General Health Insurance Company to the provider.

Part IV. Family Allowances

193. Family allowances are regulated in Act No. 117/1995 Coll. on state social support. This system was introduced in 1995, whereas previously, family benefits were spread throughout the system of social security. Some allowances for children were included in the system of sickness insurance, while some others were subject to the social care system. Conditions and concepts differed significantly from each other, and the whole range of family benefits was somewhat chaotic and therefore not as are regulated in Act No. 117/1995 Coll. on state social support. Some allowances for children were included in the system of sickness insurance; some others were subject to the social care system. Conditions and concepts differed significantly from each other, and the whole sample of family benefits was somewhat chaotic and, therefore, legally not very transparent. This problem was inherited from communist times and had to be solved by introducing a new and modern system of family benefits. The idea was to centralize the benefits, having them administered by state offices, and also to more effectively target them, through income testing, at least, in the case of some benefits.

194. During recent years, the system underwent a lot of important changes and some of its benefits were used for electoral campaigns and promises to make them more generous or to make them more effective so as to save money under the state budget.

195. Under the state social support, the following benefits are available:

- child allowance;
- housing allowance;
- parental allowance;
- birth grant;
- funeral grant.

Chapter 1. Field of Application

§1. Territorial Field of Application

196. Benefits provided from the state social support system are due to persons with residence in the territory of the Czech Republic. The entitlement conditions do not include nationality, so that benefits may be granted also to foreigners with a permanent residence permit.

197. Due to EU coordination rules, most family benefits are provided also to citizens of other EU countries or exported abroad, according to respective provisions of the coordination regulations.

§2. Personal Field of Application

198. Family benefits are provided to natural persons who meet the conditions set for each benefit differently. Generally, among the persons entitled to benefits can be people (together with their families) with permanent residence in the territory of the Czech Republic, including foreigners. Foreigners may be entitled to state social support also if they were born in the Czech territory. In the case of underage children in the territory of the Czech Republic who are entrusted to protection in place of parents' care or granted asylum, no application for permanent residence is required for the purpose of commencement of entitlement conditions.

199. For non-EU foreign nationals, registration as permanently resident in the Czech Republic is considered to be the period following the passage of 365 days from the date on which they registered to stay in the Czech Republic. This does not include any period during which a person is seeking asylum. Act No. 117/1995 Coll. on state social support stipulates other persons eligible for state social support benefits who have a residence in the Czech Republic. Within the range of persons covered, there are also EU nationals who are the subject of directly applicable EU legislation.

200. Some benefits – the so-called means-tested benefits – can be granted only if the total family income does not exceed the statutory limit. This limit is the family subsistence minimum (regulated by Act No. 110/2006 Coll.), multiplied by the relevant coefficient.

Chapter 2. Dependent Children

201. According to the current legislation in force, dependent children are children up to the end of compulsory school attendance, or beyond, if they undergo further education or vocational training or if they are disabled, but up to a maximum of 26 years of age.

202. Upon the termination of compulsory education, a child is considered dependent only under the conditions provided by Act No. 117/1995 Coll. on state social support, to the maximum age of 26 years, if:

- the child is preparing systematically for a future profession through study at a medium-grade or high-grade school; or
- the child cannot prepare systematically for a future profession or perform gainful activities because of an ailment or injury; or
- the child is unable to perform systematic gainful activities for the reason of their long-term unfavourable state of health.

203. A long-term unfavourable state of health is deemed to mean a state of health that lasts or is expected to last longer than one year. From the termination of compulsory education up until the age of 18 years, a child also registered at an RBLO as a job applicant, not entitled to unemployment support, may be considered as a dependent. However, a child drawing a full disability pension cannot be considered as dependent.

204. Child allowance is a basic long-term benefit provided to families with dependent children. A dependent child up to the age of 26 years, living in a family with an income of less than 2.4 times the family's living minimum, is entitled to this allowance. For the purposes of state social support, a family consists of parents and dependent children who reside jointly and cover the costs of their needs in common. In the case of housing allowance (*see* below), all persons registered as permanently resident in a residence are jointly assessed, and the condition of covering the costs of their needs in common is not requested.

205. Foster Child Allowance is, according to Act No. 359/1999 Coll. on social and legal protection of children, provided to dependent children placed in foster care who are entitled to an allowance. The child continues to be entitled to this allowance even after reaching adulthood, up to a maximum of 26 years of age, provided that they remain a dependent child and live under the same roof as their former foster parent(s). When foster care is ended due to the adulthood of the child, a special grant is provided to the child in order to help to start his/her independent life.

206. The grant at the end of foster care is a one-off benefit provided to young people who have grown up in foster care, reached the age of majority and are no longer eligible for the foster child allowance. This allowance is paid at a later date if such person remains a dependent child after reaching the age of majority (due to studies, etc.) and is eligible for the foster child allowance. The allowance is paid when they reach the age of 26, at the latest.

Chapter 3. Parents

207. Parents are also supported by state social support. There are some allowances and grants to which parents are entitled.

208. A childbirth grant is a one-off benefit from state social support paid in connection with childbirth. Its purpose is to help the family to cover their increased costs and also to facilitate the care of the new-born baby. Families are entitled to the birth grant provided the family income in the calendar quarter prior to the birth of the child does not exceed 2.7 times the family's living minimum. The birth grant amounts to CZK 13,000 for the first child and CZK 10,000 for the second child. The person entitled to a childbirth grant is, in the first place, the child's mother, provided she has a permanent address in the Czech Republic. The entitlement originates on the day of the childbirth. If the mother dies, it is the father of the child who is entitled to the grant, if it has not been paid yet either to the mother or to any other person. Also, a person who has taken a child of less than 1 year of age into permanent care on the basis of a decision by appropriate authority is entitled to this benefit.

209. Parental allowance may be granted to a parent who personally and duly cares for a child who is the youngest in the family until this youngest child reaches 4 years of age. Czech parental allowance is, in fact, one of the most generous benefits for parents in Europe. There is a lump-sum of CZK 220 at the disposal of parents, and in most cases, it is up to the parent to decide how fast this money will be provided.[14] The maximum monthly benefit is CZK 11,500, which means, that the parent who does not want to lose the money acquired by the parental allowance has to stay at home with the child (or work but not put the child in kindergarten for more than forty-six hours/month) for two years.[15] For people, who have earned well before they claimed the parental allowance, there is a possibility to get the maximum monthly benefit of CZK 32,600, so that the parental allowance is paid for 6 months and the parent can return to work much earlier than it is currently usual in the Czech Republic.

210. The principal purpose of a parental allowance is to contribute to the material security of the parent of a small child. For the purpose of this benefit, a person who has taken a child into permanent care is also considered as her/his parent. Such cases may concern an adopted child, a child taken into permanent care on the basis of the decision of an appropriate authority (including foster care), a child whose parent has died and the child from a former marriage of the spouse.

---

14. There are currently proposals to increase the benefit for CZK 260,000 and also to introduce the mechanism for parents who have children sooner than 4 years, one after the other, not to lose the rest of the parental allowance because a younger child is born.
15. The Government recently presented a bill, according to which, the monthly parental allowance could reach CZK 33,000, which would allow the parents who wish so to return to work after half a year.

211. The condition of all-day care is not deemed breached if a child younger than 2 years of age spends forty-six hours a month in a crèche, nursery school or some other similar institution for children of pre-school age.[16] There is no time limit for the care in an institution for children of pre-school age if the child is older than 2 years.

212. For people who have taken children into foster care, there are also special benefits legislated in Act No. 359/1999 Coll. on social and legal protection of children. There are four types of foster care benefits, three of which are provided to foster parents. Foster parent allowance may be granted to foster parents who take a child into foster care. Foster care allowance is a monthly provided benefit. A foster parent who has taken a child into foster care is entitled to a fostering grant, which is a one-off grant and has been conceptualized as a 'social remedy' for the decision to take a child into own care and to, thus, save him/her from institutional care. There is also an allowance for interim foster care. The child is placed into temporary foster care when there is a high probability that the child cannot go back to his own family after unsatisfactory conditions that caused the need for temporary foster care. These conditions can be e.g. poor social family background, serious financial problems limiting childcare, serious health 'problems of a parent, parent's addictions to alcohol or drugs. Sometimes the children, after the termination of the foster care for an interim period which is 1 year (very exceptionally 2 years), have to be fostered fully because the original family function could not be recovered. A motor vehicle grant is available for foster parents who have at least four children in foster care. Another condition of entitlement to the grant is that foster parents must not use the vehicle for occupational activities.

16. There is a proposal to abolish this condition and allow the parents of very young children to place them in a childcare facility and return to work even before the child reaches 2 years of age.

Chapter 4. Amount of the Benefit

213. The child allowance is provided on three levels, depending on the age of the child:[17]

Age of the Dependent Child	*Amount of Monthly Child Allowance in CZK*
up to 6 years of age	500
from 6 to 15 years	610
from 15 to 26 years	700

214. The amount of foster child allowance for a dependent child is settled from CZK 4,950 for a child under 6 years of age to CZK 7,260 for a child of age 18-26. If the child in foster care is a child with disabilities, the amounts increase.

215. Families are entitled to the birth grant provided the family income in the calendar quarter prior to the birth of the child does not exceed 2.7 times the family's living minimum. The birth grant amounts to CZK 13,000 for the first live-born child, CZK 10,000 for the second child.

216. Parental allowance is provided up to a total amount of CZK 220,000, at a maximum, up until 4 years of the child's age.

217. Foster parent allowance for one child is CZK 12,000 a month or CZK 18,000 if the foster parent cares for two children. A foster parent who cares for at least three foster children or at least for one child who is dependent on the care of another person, with a dependency level of II, III, or IV, is entitled to CZK 30,000 of foster parent allowance. For each additional child placed in foster care, a further amount is granted.

218. The foster parent allowance is taxed as an income from the dependent activity.

219. The amount of the motor vehicle grant depends on the price of the vehicle and may be up to 70% of its cost, with a maximum of CZK 100,000. This grant may also be provided to repair a vehicle.

17. There is a proposal to increase this benefit, it's often argued, it's too low.

Chapter 5. Payment

220. Applications for state social support benefits are handled by the contact points of the regional RBLO based on the (permanent) residence of the person entitled to the benefit (the eligible applicant).

221. Applications for benefits are submitted on forms prescribed by the Ministry of Labour and Social Affairs. The application forms are available on the internet.

222. The appeal body is the Ministry of Labour and Social Affairs.

223. Entitled to family allowances are both Czech citizens and foreigners who have a right to benefits if they and the family/household members assessed jointly with them are registered as permanently resident in the Czech Republic and have their residence there. Income in the family is decisive for entitlement to some (so-called means-tested) state social support benefits. The income under consideration includes, in particular, income from dependent activities (employment), income from entrepreneurship or other self-employment, sickness and pension scheme benefits, and unemployment benefit, including similar income from abroad. Net income is taken into account in the decisive income.

224. If the benefit is not taken, once three months have passed following the date on which the benefits apply, entitlement to the payment of that benefit is precluded. In the case of one-off benefits, entitlement expires after one year as of the date on which the benefit applies.

Part V. Incapacity to Work

225. On 12 May 2006, a new Act No. 187/2006 was published in Collection of Laws. This regulation replaces the very aged Act on sickness insurance codified in 1956, which had been effective for more than forty years in spite of the fact that the Act had been amended many times, and assignments of benefits according to it no longer reflected the social and economic development in the Czech Republic. The progressive modifications of sickness insurance were very incomprehensible and an overview could hardly be obtained. In parallel with the preparation of this Act, legislative work on modifications of other legal prescriptions with an impact on the field of sickness insurance (illness care) also proceeded. The new Act on sickness insurance was planned to come into force on 1 January 2007. Due to a short period of time between the date of publishing and the date of coming into force and due to practical problems with transposing of the new regulation to the real life, the date of coming into force was postponed twice. So, the Act finally came into force on 1 January 2009. Very important changes were brought to the system of sickness insurance during 2017 and 2018 (see below).

226. The principles of the new Act on sickness insurance can be characterized as follows:

- *complexity (codification)*, i.e., it regulates not only the participation in the sickness insurance and contributions of benefits from this insurance system but also organization and control in the field of sickness insurance, assessment of TIW by general practitioners (doctors) along with the new process of repositioning of the insured person from the class of incapacity to work to the status of invalidity, qualification and obligations of bodies in the frame of sickness insurance, obligations of employers, as well as insured persons, cases of violation in fulfilment of obligations defined by law, etc. (the legal regulation ceased to be fragmented into several Acts);
- *unification*, i.e., it shall include all insured persons regardless of the fact whether they were employees, civil servants, self-employed persons, etc.;
- *system* approach, i.e., individual parts of the legal regulation were better ordered to enable a good overview and to prevent difficult orientation in the Act.

227. Participation in sickness insurance comes true under fulfilment of conditions given by law, i.e., it is obligatory. In the case of self-employed persons, the participation in sickness insurance continues to be voluntary – it depends on the will of such persons whether they ask (apply) for participation in the insurance or not.

228. The sickness benefit, as a basic amount of money from the sickness insurance system based on illness or accident, is granted not earlier than the *fifteenth day of* 'TIW'. In the period of the first fourteen days of work incapacity, the employers pay the wage compensation to the height of 60% of average daily salary (with ceiling).

229. The benefits of sickness insurance are paid only by means of bodies in the frame of sickness insurance. Such organs are the CSSA or particularly its territorial units (DSSA), the Ministry of Defence, the Ministry of Interior and other respective institutions – the employers do not pay the benefits from sickness insurance system to their employees any more – their role is just auxiliary now.

Chapter 1. Field of Application

§1. Territorial Field of Application

230. The necessary prerequisite for the employees' participation in sickness insurance is the *performance of employment in the territory of the Czech Republic*; however, the conditions do not include the citizenship of the Czech Republic. If the employee performs temporarily her/his work outside the territory of the Czech Republic, this fact has no influence on her/his sickness insurance if the permanent place of work is situated in the territory of the Czech Republic.

231. The participation in the Czech sickness insurance system belongs also to employees who *perform their employment abroad* if:

– the registered place of business of their employer is in the territory of the Czech Republic;
– they do not have obligatory participation on sickness insurance in the state of their work; and
– their permanent residence is in the territory of the Czech Republic or of other EU Member States.

232. For the voluntary participation of self-employed persons, the territorial aspect must also be fulfilled – the self-employment must be carried out in the territory of the Czech Republic or(when the working activity is performed abroad) must be carried out on the basis of licence arising from the Czech legal order.

§2. Personal Field of Application

233. Participation in sickness insurance is one of the fundamental conditions of entitlement to sickness insurance benefits, as only the persons participating in sickness insurance are entitled to these benefits. According to the legislation in force, participation in sickness insurance is based on a certain form of working activity.

234. It applies *on an obligatory basis* to the following categories of persons (the legal regulation calls this specified group of persons as 'employees'):

– Workers with an employment relationship.
– Officers of the Police of Czech Republic, the Fire Rescue Service of Czech Republic, the Customs Administration of Czech Republic, the Prison Service of Czech Republic, the General Inspection of Security Brigades, the Security Information Service, the Office for Foreign Relations and Information, professional soldiers and soldiers with an inactive status at the time when they perform an active military service
– Civil servants under the Act on Civil Service.

- Members of cooperatives who, outside the contractual employment relationship, perform work for the cooperative for which they are remunerated by the cooperative.
- Employees performing their gainful activity on the basis of 'Agreements on Working Activity' or 'Agreement on Work Performance' (special labour law relationships different from the main employment relationship).
- Workers with an employment relationship established under foreign legislation.
- Judges.
- Members of the Boards of Representatives of territorial self-governing units and Boards of Representatives of municipal quarters or municipal districts of territorially divided statutory cities and the Capital of Prague who have been elected to functions which were determined by the Boards of Representatives as functions for which the Members of the Boards of Representatives must be disengaged from their regular occupations.
- Members of the Lower House of Parliament and Senators of the Senate of the Czech Parliament.
- Members of the government, President, Vice President and Members of the Supreme Audit Office, Members of the Council for Radio and Television Broadcasting, Members of the Board of the Office for Energetic Regulation, Members of the Board of the Institute for Studying Totalitarian Regimes, Members of the National Budget Council, Members of the Board of the Czech Telecommunication Office, Financial Arbitrator and Deputy Financial Arbitrator, Public Defender of Rights and Deputy Public Defender of Rights.
- Natural entities who, under a special law, are appointed or elected chiefs of an administrative authority or a statutory body of a legal entity established under special law, or a deputy for this chief or statutory body if this chief or statutory body is just one entity and the appointment or election did not result in establishing an employment or service relationship for these persons; natural entities who, under special law, discharge a public function outside an employment or service relationship if their employment relationship is subject to the specified scope of the Labour Code.
- Voluntary home care services staff.
- Foster parents working in facilities designed for this purpose under special legislation, or who are paid remuneration for foster care that foster parents are paid in special events and under special legislation.
- Imprisoned convicts involved in a work process.
- People working under a relationship with the same content as an employment relationship, but without establishing the employment relationship because the conditions set out by labour law for establishing an employment relationship are not met.
- Partners and executives of limited liability companies and limited partners in special limited partnerships if they carry out work for the company outside of an employment relationship, and directors of not-for-profit organizations if they carry out work for the company outside of an employment relationship.
- Authorized agents (proxies).
- Members of collective bodies of legal persons.
- Liquidators (receivers).

- Directors of branches of legal persons whose place of work is permanently situated in the Czech Republic.
- Persons delegated to perform trade management pursuant to contractual representation.
- A person not mentioned in previous points.

All these groups of persons are a party to sickness insurance when they perform an 'occupation', that means a gainful activity, if the incomes from such activity are or could be deemed incomes from dependent activity under the Income Tax Act and are not free of this tax.

235. A special sort of employees are represented by so-called contractual employees. A contractual employee is an employee of an employer whose registered office is located in a country with which the Czech Republic has not concluded the International Social Security Treaty or in a country that is not a member of the EU, nor does it use EU regulations to coordinate the social security system (hereinafter referred to as the 'foreign employer'), if such employee performs some working activity in the Czech Republic for a 'contractual employer'. A 'contractual employer' is considered to be a legal or natural entity with a registered office in the Czech Republic where the foreign employer's employees active in the Czech Republic are considered to be contractual employees in the Czech Republic if, under an agreement concluded with the foreign employer, the income of the contractual employees is paid by the contractual employer, or if the contractual employer pays this income to a foreign employer.

236. On a voluntary basis, participation in sickness insurance is possible for:

- Self-employed persons.
- Foreign employees – employees of a foreign employer if they are active in the Czech Republic for the foreign employer's benefit. Foreign employees participate in the insurance if they have applied to enter the insurance system using the prescribed form and if they have parallel participation on voluntary pension insurance.

237. She/he who performs several activities establishing her/him to the participation in sickness insurance is insured on the basis of each such activity separately.

238. From the participation in Czech sickness insurance are excluded employees performing employment in the territory of the Czech Republic for:

- an employer who enjoys diplomatic advantages and immunities if such employees are participants in insurance in another country;
- international organization if such employees are participants in insurance through the medium of this international organization, and they declare in written form to the body of sickness insurance that they want to be excluded from the Czech insurance for that reason.

239. From the participation in sickness insurance are also excluded persons who are not citizens of the Czech Republic or of the EU, and they are employed in the Czech Republic without valid entitlement to residence in the territory of the Czech Republic under a special law.

240. Exempted from participation in sickness insurance are the employees performing so-called short-range employment – employment concluded with monthly income lower than the decisive income of CZK 2,500 (this amount will increase to CZK 3,000 from 2019); such employment establishes participation in the sickness insurance only in the calendar month in which at least the amount of decisive income was eventually accounted (e.g., as a result of some extraordinary remuneration). Such employees are also participants in sickness insurance if they carry out work for the same employer on the basis of more 'short-range employments' and the sum of their creditable earnings from such agreements reaches the decisive income per calendar month. Similar rules are also valid for persons working on the basis of 'Agreement on Work Performance', but the decisive income represents CZK 10,000 (*see* below).

§3. The Origin of the Participation in Insurance

I. Wage-Earners

241. Sickness insurance is usually established by the start of performing employment and terminated by the end of employment. The precondition for participating in sickness insurance is working in the Czech Republic in a job carried out under a contractual employment relationship or an employment relationship which may establish participation in this insurance (*see* above). Another precondition is the minimum amount of the agreed income (what is known as the 'decisive income', the level of which has been set at CZK 2,500, and will be raised according to average wage developments – from 2019 the amount is at CZK 3,000).

242. Persons working on the basis of an 'agreement on work performance' are participants in sickness insurance in calendar months in which they have received an amount of creditable incomes which exceeds CZK 10,000. Such employees are also participants in sickness insurance if they carry out work for the same employer on the basis of more 'agreements on work performance' and the sum of their creditable earnings from such agreements exceeds CZK 10,000 per calendar month.

243. In the case that a respective 'social event' arises by a person who performs a 'short-range employment' or employment on the basis of an 'agreement on work performance' in a calendar month in which the 'decisive income' was not reached, such a person shall not acquire the right to respective benefit. Anyway, the sickness benefit or maternity benefit belongs to such person in case that the temporary incapacity to work arises or the accession to the maternity benefit begins in a calendar month which follows immediately a period of three months of uninterrupted participation in sickness insurance.

244. If these conditions are fulfilled, the participation in sickness insurance usually originates to the day in which the employee began to perform the working activity for the employer and expires on the day of ending of 'occupation period' (that means to the end of the period within which the working activity should be or could be performed). Anyway there are some specific forms of employment (Contractual employees, Judges, Members of the Boards of Representatives of territorial self-governing units, Members of the Lower House of Parliament and Senators of the Senate of the Czech Parliament, foster parents, imprisoned convicts involved in a work process, partners and executives, liquidators, persons delegated to perform trade management) for which the special rules for determination of the exact day of origin and expiry of participation in sickness insurance are laid down.

II. Self-Employed

245. For the self-employed persons, the participation in sickness insurance is voluntary. The self-employed person participates in sickness insurance only if she/he has submitted an application for participation in sickness insurance on the required form. The concrete day of origin of participation in sickness insurance is set in the application – the self-employed person is entitled to choose such day, but it cannot pre-date the day of submission of the application. She/he who performs several self-employments at the same time is insured only once. In case that the self-employed person is not applied for such participation, she/he is not entitled to enjoy benefits from the reason of illness/sickness or pregnancy/maternity. However, even the insured self-employed person is never entitled to enjoy the 'attendance allowance' or 'compensatory benefit in pregnancy and maternity' (*see* below).

246. In the text which follows, the wage-earners and the self-employed persons are not treated separately, as the legislation for both categories is very similar. We shall only point to the differences in the respective chapters.

Chapter 2. Incapacity to Work (General Information)

§1. Incapacity to Work: Definition and Consequences

247. 'Incapacity to work' in the sense of the Czech social security system can be generally defined as *the impossibility to perform a gainful activity as from the reason(s) related to health sphere of natural person* (illness, pregnancy, childbirth and maternity, paternity). In most cases, the health problem is on side of the beneficiary of respective statutory benefit, the law of sickness insurance also deals with situations when the beneficiary temporarily provides care to somebody who suffers from health problems (*see* below the benefit called 'attendance allowance' or 'long-term care allowance').

248. To the injured person, the incapacity to work also brings problems in the economic (income) sphere – such a person is unable to earn money by herself/himself because her/his health status does not allow this – we talk about so-called unfavourable health status. The task of 'social insurance' is to solve these economic consequences and the 'unfavourable health status'. In the sphere of financing of necessary healthcare, the system of health insurance plays a privileged role.

249. The nature of the 'incapacity to work' can be 'temporary' or 'permanent'. The system of sickness insurance is meant to solve the consequences of TIW (short-term illness, pregnancy, childbirth and maternity, paternity, short-term or medium-term need to take care of someone). If the incapacity to work as a result of unfavourable health status becomes permanent (serious long-term illness or accident with irreversible consequences), the health status of such a person is designated as 'invalidity' and the benefits for invalid persons are provided from the system of pension insurance (*see* below the 'invalidity pension').

§2. Certification of 'TIW'

250. The TIW is considered to be the condition which, for health disorders or other reasons laid down by this Act, does not enable the insured person to perform the existing insured activities and, if the health disorder lasts for longer than 180 calendar days, does not enable the insured person to perform other than the existing insured activities. If, after the elapse of 180 calendar days of the TIW, the insured person can perform activities other than the existing insured ones, i.e., to comply with the requirements for job seekers, the TIW shall be terminated.

251. The TIW is certified by an 'attending physician', in special cases by the DSSA through its own physician. For the purpose of this certification, the 'attending physician' is deemed to mean the medical institution which, through its own physicians, provides to insured persons or other persons ambulatory, institutional or spa care.

252. The TIW is certified most frequently when the physician ascertains by examination that the person's 'health status' does not permit her/him to perform her/his employment or gainful activities. However, in some special enumerated cases, the TIW can be certified even if condition stated in the previous sentence was not fulfilled (fiction of the TIW is the necessary precondition of the entitlement for the benefit).

253. The physician certifies the TIW on a prescribed form which becomes the document of incapacity to work. This document contains the identification of the person incapacitated to work, the report to her/his employer, possibly to the respective Labour Office on the start of TIW, the report on the termination of the TIW, and the report to the respective DSSA. The document on TIW is intended for entitlement to sickness benefits, for the files of incapacitated persons and for the employer to excuse the incapacitated employee from work. The attending physician sends to the appropriate DSSA the documents on the start of TIW and its termination, at the latest, on a working day following the day on which they have been issued. The DSSA are entitled to supervise the assessment of TIW through their own physicians.

254. Entitlement to benefits in case of the existing TIW is applied by the submission of the prescribed form issued by the respective physician. The employees submit the form to their employer, the self-employed to the DSSA.

255. The employer or later (from the employer's impulse) the respective DSSA (*see* below) pays the benefits in the cases of statutory entitlement or stops their payment when it becomes obvious that the conditions of entitlement are no longer complied with. For self-employed persons, the competent body to pay the 'sickness benefit' is also the DSSA (from the fifteenth day of the 'TIW').

256. During the existence of the TIW, the beneficiary (of the 'wage compensation' or of the 'sickness benefit') is obliged to submit himself/herself to the 'temporary-incapable-to-work regime'. The 'attending physician' determines the strict rules of therapy, the place where the therapy shall be realized and the range of time when the sick person is allowed to leave the place of therapy (so-called 'walks'). The fact whether the beneficiary complies with the rules of the regime is being accidentally controlled by the employer or DSSA. To the person who breaks the rules of this regime, the benefit can be shortened or suspended; if the violation is serious, her/his employment relationship can be legally terminated.

257. For the purposes of other 'sickness insurance benefits', the physicians also determine the 'expected date of birth' or the fact that there is an objective need (necessity) to take care of (attend to) the child or another family member. From 1 June 2018, special competencies have been laid down by 'hospitals' to certify that there is a need of 'long-term care' for the purposes of 'long-term care allowance' and consecutive competencies of 'attending physicians' to certify that such a need still lasts.

Chapter 3. Benefits

§1. Wage-Earners

258. The number of pecuniary benefits paid from the system of sickness insurance includes:

(1) Sickness benefit
(2) Attendance allowance
(3) Long-term care allowance
(4) Maternity benefit
(5) Compensatory benefit in pregnancy and maternity
(6) The benefit of fatherly post-partum care (abb. 'paternity benefit').

I. Sickness Benefit

259. The 'sickness benefit' is provided to persons whose health status corresponds to 'TIW'. The sense of the benefit is to compensate for the lapse of incomes caused by this specific 'social event'.

260. Since the new Act No. 187/2006 Coll. on sickness insurance has been in force, the 'sickness benefit' under this Act is not provided right from the beginning of the 'TIW'. For the first fourteen calendar days, the costs of such 'social event' are shared by the employer – he provides to the employee the 'wage compensation' under the respective provisions of the Labour Code. This compensation is provided per working day. The employee shall only be entitled to the compensation wage for the period of the employment relationship that establishes the participation in sickness insurance.

261. Only if the 'TIW' lasts longer than fourteen days, the obligation of the DSSA to pay the 'sickness benefit' arises. This benefit also belongs to people who are obliged to subject themselves to quarantine ordered by a respective authority under the special legislation.

262. The entitlement to 'sickness benefit' does not belong to persons who:

- have intentionally incurred a 'TIW';
- are entitled to enjoy the payment of old-age pension if the insured activity has ended before the day of such pension's award;
- sustained a 'TIW' or were ordered into quarantine while escaping from a place of custody or imprisonment.

263. The 'period of support' lasts no longer than 380 calendar days from the date of origin of the 'TIW' or quarantine order, unless stated otherwise. After the elapse of the main 'period of support', the payment of 'sickness benefit' can continue, at most, for another 350 calendar days only if the body of sickness insurance (DSSA) decides so; the necessary precondition of such decision is an assessment of the physician of DSSA that there is a chance for repair of health status within this extended period of time.

264. Those who receive 'old-age pension' or 'third-stage invalidity pension' are also entitled to enjoy the payment of the 'sickness benefit' from the fifteenth calendar day of their 'TIW' or from the fifteenth calendar day of the quarantine. However, their 'period of support' is no longer than seventy calendar days and lasts, at most, to the end of the insured activity.

II. Attendance Allowance

265. The right to enjoy 'attendance allowance' belongs to an 'employee' who cannot perform a gainful activity because she/he needs to attend to (take care of):

- a child younger than 10 years if this child has turned ill or suffered an injury;
- another member of the employee's household whose health status is unfavourable;
- a healthy child younger than 10 years because the school or other child facility has been closed (due to a breakdown, epidemic, another unforeseen event), the child has been ordered into quarantine, or the person who otherwise takes care of the child has fallen ill.

266. An employee is not entitled to 'attendance allowance' for attending to or taking care of a child if another natural entity is, on the grounds of taking care of the child, entitled to receive maternity benefit or entitled to parental benefits; this does not apply if the other person has fallen ill, sustained an injury, is in situations set out by law, borne a child or been ordered into quarantine, and for this reason such another person cannot take care of the child.

267. In the same case of attendance, the attendance allowance is only paid to one of the entitled persons or to two entitled persons, subsequently, if they change each other in the same case of attendance. Such a change is possible only once.

268. Some groups of insured persons are not entitled to the 'attendance allowance' (e.g., employees performing short-range employment).

269. The 'period of support' for the attendance allowance is no longer than nine calendar days. If an employee who permanently takes care of at least one child younger than 16 years of age who has not finished compulsory education and lives alone, the 'period of support' is extended to sixteen calendar days. The 'period of support' is suspended if the beneficiary of care was consigned to the care of some healthcare institution.

III. Long-Term Care Allowance

270. The right to enjoy 'long-term care allowance' belongs to the insured person who takes care of a person whose health status requires the need for long-term care in a domestic environment, if such an insured person in the period of care does not perform any employment or self-employment. It is necessary that the 'person who needs long-term care' has given to the insured person written permission to provide him/her the care and that such permission was not recalled.

271. As a 'person who needs long-term care' for these purposes is considered a natural person by which

– such a serious health disorder appeared, which required hospitalization and healthcare for at least seven successive calendar days (including the day of such a person's admission to the hospital and the day of his/her discharge from the hospital)
– there is a supposition, that his/her health status after the discharge from the hospital to the domestic environment will necessarily need providing long-term care for a period of at least 30 calendar days.

272. The right to enjoy 'long-term care allowance' belongs to the insured person only if such a person is in any of these relations to the 'person who needs long term care':

– his/her wife/husband or registered partner or partner or another natural person sharing a joint household with him/her;
– a direct-line relative (direct ascendant or descendant), sibling, father-in-law, mother-in-law, son-in-law, daughter-in-law, niece, nephew, aunt, uncle, or husband/wife, registered partner or partner of any of these relative persons.

273. Another condition for entitlement is at least 90 calendar days of participation in sickness insurance within 4 months immediately foregoing the day of origin of the need of long-term care or the day of taking over of such care. For self-employed persons (or 'foreign employees') there is a need for a whole 3 months of participation in sickness insurance immediately foregoing the day of origin of the need for long-term care or the day of taking over of such care.

274. The entitlement to 'long-term care allowance' shall arise again no sooner than after the lapse of 12 months from the last day of the previous entitlement to this benefit, within the same need for long-term care.

275. Some groups of insured persons are not entitled to the 'long-term care allowance' (e.g., employees performing 'short-range employment' or employment on the basis of 'agreement on work performance'). An insured person is not entitled to 'long-term care allowance' for attending to or taking care of a child if another natural entity is, on the grounds of taking care of the child, entitled to receive maternity benefit or entitled to parental benefits; this does not apply if the other person has fallen ill, sustained an injury, is in situations set out by law, has had a child or has been ordered into quarantine, and from this reason such another person cannot take care of the child.

276. In the case that there are more persons providing long-term care to a person who needs such care, the 'long-term care allowance' belongs only once and only to one of the persons taking care or, subsequently, to more persons if they change within the period of taking care.

277. The 'period of support' for the 'long-term care allowance' is no longer than 90 calendar days. The period starts on the day of origin of the need for long-term care and ends on the day when such a need terminates. There are some situations laid down by law when the 'long-term care allowance' is not provided even if the need for 'long-term care' still lasts.

IV. Maternity Benefit (Pecuniary Assistance in Maternity)

278. The 'maternity benefit' belongs to:

- an insured woman who has given birth to a child; the benefit, however, belongs to the pregnant insured woman already before the childbirth, namely, at the earliest from the beginning of the eighth week before the 'expected day of childbirth' (appointed by a gynaecologist);
- an insured person who undertook a child to 'care supplying the care of parents' on the basis of a decision of a respective body (court, administrative authority);
- an insured person who takes care of a child whose mother has died;
- an insured man who takes care of the child as her/his father or a husband of a woman who has given birth to the child, if the child's mother (who is not entitled to enjoy the 'maternity benefit') is unable or not allowed to take care of the child because of a serious long-term illness;
- an insured man who takes care of the child as her/his father or a husband of woman who has given birth to the child, if he has concluded an agreement on such care with the child's mother (such agreement can be concluded, at the earliest, from the beginning of the seventh week to after the day of childbirth and must include data laid down by law).

279. The necessary precondition of the entitlement to the 'maternity benefit' is that the insured person must have participated in the sickness insurance system *for at least 270 calendar days,* within the last two years, before the date of beginning the maternity leave, to have the right to this benefit. The period of participation in sickness insurance includes:

- the period of studies at a secondary school, vocational college or university considered to be the 'systematic preparation for a future profession' for the purposes of pension insurance, if the study was terminated successfully;

- the period of enjoying of the 'third-stage invalidity pension' if the pension was suspended and after the suspension, the insured activity originated or continued.

280. The 'maternity benefit' shall be provided from the time of commencement of 'maternity leave' according to the Labour Code. The time of commencement is understood as:

- the day determined by the pregnant woman herself whereas such date shall fall within the period between the beginning of the eighth and the beginning of the sixth week prior to the 'expected date of birth'; if the insured woman does not determine such a date during this period, the administration of the 'maternity benefit' starts from the beginning of the sixth week prior to the 'expected date of birth';
- the date of the childbirth, if the childbirth occurs prior to the time of commencement of maternity leave;
- the day of taking care, if the care was taken over by a person other than the mother who has given birth to the child.

281. The 'support period' for the 'maternity benefit' begins with the start of the maternity leave (no later than the beginning of the sixth week before the 'expected date of childbirth'), and makes:

- twenty-eight weeks for an insured woman who has given birth to a child (even if she is an employee who is not married, is widowed, divorced, or alone for other serious reasons);
- thirty-seven weeks for an insured woman who has given birth to two or more children at the same time, whereas after twenty-eight weeks of the support period, the 'maternity benefit' belongs only if the insured woman continues to take care of at least two of these children;
- twenty-two weeks for an insured person who took over the care of the child (person different from the mother who has given birth to a child);
- thirty-one weeks for an insured person who took over the care of more children (person different from the mother who has given birth to a child) whereas after twenty-two weeks of the support period, the 'maternity benefit' belongs only if the insured beneficiary continues to take care of at least two of these children.

282. The payment of the 'maternity benefit' can be interrupted in special statutory cases (e.g., when the child is entrusted to care of some medical institution and the beneficiary of the benefit begins to perform the insured activity).

V. Compensatory Benefit in Pregnancy and Maternity

283. Under Article 29 of the Charter of Fundamental Rights and Freedoms, women are entitled to special health protection at work and to special working conditions. Pregnant women are guaranteed special care, protection in employment relations and adequate working conditions (Article 32, paragraph 2 of the Constitutional Charter).

284. The 'compensatory benefit in pregnancy and maternity' is provided to a female employee who was 'transferred to a different work position' because of her pregnancy and maternity whereas as a result of this transfer she receives a lower income without a fault of her own. The reason for the 'transfer to a different work position' under the Labour Code was the fact that such an employee had performed a work which is not allowed to be performed by pregnant women or mothers under the special legislation. This also applies to female employees who cannot perform their current work because it would, according to a statement of their physician, pose a risk to their pregnancy, motherhood or breastfeeding.

285. The benefit is provided to a pregnant employee or the mother of a child, at most, until the end of the ninth month after the childbirth. The benefit is provided for the number of calendar days that the 'transfer to a different work position' lasted. To the pregnant employee, the benefit is paid, at most, up to the start of the sixth week prior to the expected date of birth. During maternity, the benefit is provided, at most, up to the end of the ninth month following birth and to breastfeeding women for the period of their breastfeeding.

286. The benefit is not provided in special statutory cases (e.g., when the beneficiary was found 'temporarily incapable to work' or when she is on maternity or parental leave under the Labour Code).

VI. 'Paternity Benefit' (Benefit of Fatherly Post-Partum Care)

287. 'Paternity benefit' belongs to:

- an insured man who takes care of the children whose father he is;
- an insured man who undertook a child to 'care supplying the care of parents' on the basis of a decision of a respective body (court, administrative authority) if the child to the day of its taking-over to such care has not reached 7 years of age.

288. The necessary precondition of the entitlement to the 'paternity benefit' for a 'self-employed' man (or 'foreign employee') is his participation in sickness insurance for a whole 3 months immediately foregoing the day of his/her accession to the father's benefit.

289. The 'paternity benefit' belongs only if the accession to this benefit arose within the period of six weeks from the childbirth or from its taking-over to care.

290. In the case that the insured man takes care of more children born at the same time or of more children which were taken-over at the same time, the 'paternity benefit belongs to such an insured man only once.

291. The 'support period' for the paternity benefit is one week long. The accession to this benefit begins from the day which is determined by the insured person; such day must fall within a period of 6 weeks from the day when the child was born or taken-over. The 'support period' shall not interrupt. The benefit belongs for the whole length of the 'support period' even in the case that the child dies before the lapse of 'support period'.

§2. Self-Employed Workers

292. Even though some of the above-mentioned rules are applied for self-employed persons, by this category of workers some special aberrations come across. These aberrations are related to their voluntary participation in sickness insurance on one side and to the special nature of their gainful activity on the other side.

293. From the above-stated enumeration of benefits, the self-employed persons are (by meeting all the statutory conditions) only entitled to enjoy:

- sickness benefit;
- long-term care allowance;
- maternity benefit (pecuniary assistance in maternity);
- 'paternity benefit.

294. The other two benefits are only provided to employees.

295. The self-employed person is entitled to *sickness benefit* if she/he has been found 'temporarily incapable to work', or has been put to quarantine if such social event lasts longer than fourteen calendar days. Another necessary precondition of their entitlement to the benefit is (in contrast to employees) some minimum period of participation in insurance prior to the origin of the social event – the minimum statutory length of this period is three months immediately preceding the day of the origin of the incapacity (quarantine). A self-employed person also must not personally perform a gainful activity during the time of the incapacity (quarantine). These are probably the reasons why many self-employed persons are not interested in voluntary participation in sickness insurance.

296. As the *long-term care allowance* regards, there is also the condition that the entitled person does not perform his/her self-employment. Further, there is a need for a whole 3 months of participation in sickness insurance immediately foregoing the day of origin of the need for long-term care or the day of taking-over of such care.

297. As the *maternity benefit* (pecuniary assistance in maternity) regards, the self-employed person also must not personally perform gainful activity. The period of participation in the sickness insurance system must be at least 180 days during one year prior to the day when the payment of 'maternity benefit' started (and besides this, the general condition of 270 calendar days during the last two years before the first day of the payment must be fulfilled).

298. In the case of the *'paternity benefit,* there is also a need for participation in sickness insurance for a whole 3 months immediately foregoing the day of his/her accession to the father's benefit.

§3. Funeral Benefit

299. Analogously, with the childbirth grant until 30 September 1995, the funeral benefits were pecuniary (cash) benefits of sickness insurance of employees or sickness care in armed forces. At the present time, the funeral benefits, similarly as the childbirth grants, are pecuniary (cash) benefits provided from the system of state social support under Act No. 117/1995 Coll. on state social support as amended.

300. One of the specific situations, the solution of which is participated in by the state, is the funeral. Stricter entitlement conditions introduced by the above-mentioned Act include testing whether the deceased had a permanent residence in the territory of the Czech Republic at the time of death; otherwise, the entitlement to the benefit does not originate.

301. The entitlement originates on the day of the funeral. The amount of the benefit is at present CZK 5,000 and is paid as a lump-sum. Funeral benefit belongs only to the person who had organized a funeral to an 'unprovided' child or to the parent of an 'unprovided' child.

Chapter 4. Amount of the Benefits

302. The amount of the benefit is fully dependent on the amount of the so-called daily calculation base. First of all, the entire sum of calculation basis (for the contribution to the system of the sickness insurance) per 'decisive period' is divided by the number of calendar days falling within the 'decisive period' (twelve calendar months prior to the calendar month of origin of the respective social event). If there exist some 'excluded periods' (the periods when the activity was not performed, e.g., when the insured person was 'incapable to work'), these periods are not included in the number of calendar days falling within the 'decisive period'.

303. Such determined 'real daily average of incomes' (calculation bases) is reduced consequently as follows:

- For the 'sickness benefit', 'attendance allowance' and the 'long-term care allowance': 90% up to the amount of the first 'reduction level'; 60% from the amount exceeding the first reduction level up to the second reduction level; 30% from the amount exceeding the second reduction level up to the third reduction level; and the amount above the third reduction level is not taken into account.
- For the 'maternity benefit', paternity benefit and the 'compensatory benefit in pregnancy and maternity': 100% up to the amount of the first reduction level; 60% from the amount exceeding the first reduction level up to the second reduction level; 30% from the amount exceeding the second reduction level up to the third reduction level; and the amount above the third reduction level is not taken into account.

304. The 'reduction levels' change every calendar year due to the evolvement of the 'average state wages'. The amount of them is declared every year by special ordinance of the Ministry of Labour and Social Affairs in the Collection of Acts. For 2018, the following amounts are valid:

(1) First reduction level – CZK 1000.
(2) Second reduction level – CZK 1,499.
(3) Third reduction level – CZK 2,998.

305. The result of this calculation is the 'daily calculation base'. The amount of the individual benefit shall be determined as a percentual part of the 'daily calculation base'. The daily amount of:

- 'Sickness benefit' makes:
  a) 60 % of the 'daily calculation base' (similar rule is applied by the 'wage compensation' which is, however, provided per working day) within a period of first 30 days of duration of TIW (quarantine),
  b) 66 % of the 'daily calculation base' within a period from 31st day to 60th day of duration of TIW (quarantine),

c) 72 % of the 'daily calculation base' within a period from 61st day of duration of TIW (quarantine) to the end of the TIW (quarantine) or to the end of 'support period';
d) 100 % of the 'daily calculation base' within a whole period of duration of TIW (quarantine) in case that the TIW (quarantine) arose (was ordered) as a consequence of the fact that an insured person in the public interest, provably, had taken part in fire-fighting, in providing of rescue or liquidating works or in fulfilling tasks of inhabitant-security as a member of volunteer fire company (brigade).

– 'Attendance Allowance' makes 60% of the 'daily calculation base'.
– 'Long-term Care Allowance' makes 60% of the 'daily calculation base'.
– 'Maternity Benefit' makes 70% of the 'daily calculation base'.
– 'Compensatory benefit in pregnancy and maternity' makes the amount of the 'odds' between the 'daily calculation base' ascertained to the day of 'transfer to a different work position' and the average daily income after this transfer.
– 'Paternity benefit' makes 70% of the 'daily calculation base'.

306. In the case that the 'TIW' was caused by its beneficiary's involvement in a fight or as a direct consequence of being drunk or having misused narcotics or psychotropic substances, or while committing an intentional crime or intentionally committed offence, such person is only entitled to enjoy 50% of the 'sickness benefit' per calendar day.

Chapter 5. Protection Period

307. All the sickness benefits are granted *per calendar day*, i.e., from the first calendar day of the entitlement to its termination (including weekends and statutory holidays).

308. The necessary precondition of the entitlement to all the benefits is the *existing participation in the sickness* insurance *to the day of the origin of the respective social event.* However, the legal regulations allow (in enumerated cases – 'sickness benefit', 'maternity benefit') to reach the entitlement to statutory benefits to the persons who, at the moment of the origin of the social event, are not such participants – the entitlement can be admitted even if the social event arises within the so-called protection period.

309. The 'protection period' shall be calculated from the day which follows the day when the participation in the sickness insurance had terminated. By the:

- 'sickness benefit', the 'protection period' makes at the most *7 calendar days*;
- 'maternity benefit', the protection period makes at the most *180 calendar days* for women whose insurance had terminated during pregnancy; in other cases, the 'protection period' makes at the most *7 calendar days.*

310. If the entire period of the person's participation in sickness insurance was shorter than the statutory length of the 'protection period' (7 days, 180 days), the length of the 'protection period' is as long as the length of such participation.

311. The 'protection period' is not provided:

- on the grounds of insured activities of a beneficiary of the 'old-age pension' or of the 'third-stage invalidity pension';
- on the grounds of other employment, i.e., employment concluded only for the period corresponding to the period of recreational leave drawn from the primary employment;
- on the grounds of the 'short-range employment';
- on the grounds of employment concluded by an insured person who is a pupil or student if the employment is only concluded for the period of school holidays or holidays in general;
- in case that the insurance of a convicted person terminates at the time of her/his escape from the place of imprisonment;
- on the grounds of employment performed on the basis of 'Agreement on Work Performance';
- on the grounds of active military service of a soldier with an inactive status;
- on the grounds of remunerated activity related to liability for service.

312. The insured person is not entitled to enjoy the benefit if she/he performs work in the insured activity on the grounds of which the benefit is provided or performs the self-employment personally.

313. The entitlement to the payment of the 'sickness benefit', the 'attendance allowance', the 'long-term care allowance', the 'maternity benefit', the paternity benefit and the 'compensatory benefit in pregnancy and maternity' expires, if not claimed within three years from the day on which it has been due.

Part VI. Industrial Accidents and Occupational Diseases

314. As the new codification of accident insurance (Act No. 266/2006 Coll. on accident insurance) in the Czech Republic was abolished even before it entered into force, the main source of the legislation on accident insurance is the Labour Code (Act No. 262/2006 Coll.), even if the Labour Code does not provide for a complex system but, rather provisionally, responds to the need of social security provided to employees in case of an industrial accident or an occupational disease.

315. At the end of the 1950s, industrial accident insurance was abolished in former Czechoslovakia and employees' entitlements were conceived as compensation for damages. The damage was represented as the difference between average earnings and sickness insurance benefits or subsequent earnings (achieved after the accident) with the addition of full or partial disability pension. The damages did not represent high amounts for the then state enterprises but would represent considerable expenditure for present-day private enterprises. Therefore, the 1992 Labour Code amendment introduced obligatory statutory liability insurance, at that time run exclusively by one insurance company (Czech Insurance Company), some years later accompanied by another private insurance company – Kooperativa. Both subjects are defined by the law as exclusive administrators of the system.

316. For the purpose of the Pension Insurance Act (which is of significance regarding entitlement to disability pension, or survivors pensions), an industrial accident is deemed to mean an accident considered an industrial or service accident under labour law regulations or regulations concerning service relations. Also, some other enumerated accidents (during preparations for the defence of the Czech Republic, during service in armed forces, etc.) are considered industrial accidents. The same approach applies to occupational diseases also.

Chapter 1. Field of Application

§1. Territorial Field of Application

317. The employer with whom the employee has been in an employment relationship at the time of the accident is always liable for damage due to an industrial accident, regardless of where the accident has taken place (whether in the Czech Republic or abroad). The last employer, for whom the employee worked before the ascertainment of the occupational disease in an employment relationship under the conditions giving rise to the occupational disease, is liable for the damage caused to the employee by the acquired occupational disease.

§2. Personal Field of Application

318. The Labour Code (Part 11) grants entitlement to compensation of damages due to an industrial accident or occupational disease which applies to any employee, who suffered by an industrial accident or occupational disease in connection with performing her/his working activity. Labour liability also applies to civil servants (according to section 124 of Act No. 234/2014 Coll. on civil service).

Chapter 2. Concept of 'Industrial Accident'

§1. Accident

319. An industrial accident occurs if an accident which caused damage to the health of an employee or the death of an employee occurred during the fulfilment of working tasks or in direct relation thereto. The Labour Code does not define the concept of accident; its definition by means of the action resulting in it can be found only in adjudications, and according to the decisions of Czech courts, it is deemed to involve a sudden and forceful effect of external factors on the corporeal or psychic integrity of an employee or another natural person.

§2. Link to the Contract of Employment

320. The origin of liability for damages caused by an industrial accident or an occupational disease assumes the conclusion of a labour contract or the existence of an employment relationship. According to section 269 of the Labour Code the employer must compensate the employee, damages or non-pecuniary damage, who suffered an accident at work, if the loss or damage was caused when fulfilling work tasks or in direct connection with it. The employer is also obliged to compensate the employee damages or non-pecuniary damage resulting from occupational disease if the employee last worked before detection by the employer under conditions in which there is an occupational disease, which has been affected. The fulfilment of working tasks or direct connection therewith are not defined by the Labour Code but there are some implementation regulations, as well as the settled case law of the national courts.

321. The fulfilment of working tasks is the performance of working obligations arising from the employment relationship, other activities performed upon the employer's order and activities forming the object of a business trip. The fulfilment of working tasks also includes activities performed for the employer on the instruction of the trade union organization, employees' council, possibly their representative for occupational safety and health protection at work or other employees, and possibly also activities for the employer performed on the employee's own initiative, if they do not require special authority or if not performed against the employer's express prohibition, as well as voluntary assistance organized by the employer. Direct connection with the fulfilment of working tasks includes those activities required for work performance and activities customary or necessary before the start of work or after its termination, as well as activities customary at the time of break for food and rest performed on the employer's premises. Activities directly connected with the fulfilment of working tasks are deemed to also include training courses organized for employees by the employer or a trade union organization (section 274 of the Labour Code). Also, an accident suffered by an employee due to the fulfilment of his working tasks is considered an industrial accident.

§3. ACCIDENTS ON THE WAY TO WORK

322. An accident suffered by an employee on the way to work and back is not considered an industrial accident, according to section 271k of the Labour Code. The way to work and back is deemed to mean travel from the employee's domicile to the place intended for the fulfilment of the employee's working task and back.

323. However, travel from the municipality of the employee's domicile to the worksite or to her/his accommodation in another municipality which is the target of her/his business trip, unless it is simultaneously to the municipality of her/his regular worksite, and back, is considered as a necessary activity before the start of the work or after its termination; an accident suffered in this way is, hence, considered an industrial accident (section 274a of the Labour Code).

Chapter 3. Concept of 'Occupational Disease'

324. Occupational diseases are diseases specified in social security regulations if they have originated under the conditions specified therein. The specific regulation is Order of the Government No. 290/1995 Coll. providing the list of occupational diseases. These are diseases originating from the adverse effect of chemical, physical, biological or other detrimental factors if they have originated under the conditions specified in the list of occupational diseases which are included as an annexe to the above-mentioned order. The term 'occupational disease' also includes acute poisoning originating from the adverse effect of chemical agents. Also, a disease which originated before its inclusion in the list of occupational diseases may be compensated as an occupational disease from the date of its inclusion in the list for the maximum period of three years before the inclusion.

325. The assessment and certification of occupational diseases is performed by special medical institutions specifically intended for this purpose (specified in the Ordinance of the Ministry of Health No. 104/2012 Coll., which sets out the procedure of certification of occupational diseases and issues the list of medical institutions certifying these diseases) on the basis of an assessment by a medical institution comprising a department or clinic of occupational diseases or occupational medicine.

Chapter 4. Medical Care

326. Employees who have suffered an industrial accident or have been found to suffer from an occupational disease are granted medical (preventative) care under Act No. 372/2011 Coll. and the Public Health Insurance Act (Act No. 48/1997 Coll.). This care comprises the care of health restoration and strengthening, and includes all ambulatory, as well as institutional care including professional urgent pre-hospitalization care (provided by the first-aid service), diagnostic care, rehabilitation, spa treatment, provision of medicines, therapeutic and orthopaedic aids, and other means of medical technology and transport of the patient. It also includes preventative care provided by the employer including dispensary examinations of persons suffering from occupational diseases and persons affected by occupational risks even after they have ceased to be exposed to these risks. Detailed information has been provided above in the section on healthcare and its regulation.

327. If the state of injury or disease requires care which cannot be provided to the wounded or sick person by ambulatory services, she/he is granted institutional care in a hospital as a rule, or possibly in a specialized therapeutic institution. Spa treatment is provided to persons suffering from occupational diseases and other damage to health due to work provided this has been recommended or if its indication has been confirmed by a specialist in occupational diseases.

328. The costs of healthcare services provided due to industrial accident or occupational disease are usually paid from accident insurance by the competent insurance company.

Chapter 5. Incapacity to Work

329. Incapacity to work caused by an industrial accident or an occupational disease is assessed under general regulations on sickness insurance. A physician certifies a citizen unfit for work if he ascertains by an examination that her/his state of health, due to illness or injury, does not permit her/him to perform her/his employment or self-employment gainful activities. Under the conditions specified in Act No. 187/2006 Coll. on sickness insurance of employees, a citizen temporarily certified as incapacitated due to the performance of his employment is entitled to sickness benefits.

330. Sickness benefit is a pecuniary (cash) sickness insurance benefit granted from the twenty-first calendar day of incapacity to work until its termination or the award of a disability pension, maximally, however, for one year from the start of incapacity to work. From the third until the twentieth day of incapacity to work, it is the employer who is liable for the payment of compensation to their own employee. The conditions of compensation are regulated in sections 192–194 of the Labour Code. Detailed information has been provided above in the section on sickness insurance and its regulation.

331. If an employee who has suffered an industrial accident or who has been found to suffer from an occupational disease has been certified as disabled for these reasons, according to section 271d of the Labour Code, the employer is obliged to grant him compensation for the loss of earnings following the termination of the period of incapacity to work in the scope in which the employer is liable for the damage. This compensation is granted to the employee to the amount which, together with his earnings after the industrial accident or discovery of the occupational disease, possibly with the addition of a disability pension granted for the same reasons, will make her/his total income equal her/his mean earnings before the origin of the damage. The employee is entitled to compensation for the loss of earnings, maximally, until the end of the calendar month in which she/he attains 65 years of age.

Chapter 6. Death

332. If an employee dies as a result of an industrial accident or an occupational disease, according to section 271g–271j of the Labour Code, the employer is obliged to provide, within the scope of his liability:

- compensation for costs reasonably expended on her/his medical treatment;
- compensation for reasonable expenses connected with the funeral;
- compensation for sustenance costs of the survivors;
- ad hoc indemnification of survivors;
- compensation for material damage.

333. The employee's death annuls his entitlement to compensation for pain (smart-money) and the aggravation of social assertion.

334. Costs connected with medical treatment and costs connected with a funeral are refunded to the person who has expended them. The sum of funeral costs is reduced by the deduction of the funeral grant granted under the State Social Support Act (Act No. 117/1995 Coll., as amended). Compensation for the costs of a tombstone or a slab is granted up to CZK 20,000, at the least (section 271g of the Labour Code). Compensation for the survivors' sustenance costs is due to those survivors to whom the deceased provided or was obliged to provide sustenance unless this compensation is covered by pension benefits paid for the same reason.

335. Ad hoc indemnification is due to the spouse and a child. In substantiated cases, it is also granted to the parents of the deceased employee. The amount of compensation is at least CZK 240,000 (section 271i of the Labour Code).

Chapter 7. Prevention of Occupational Diseases and Industrial Accidents

336. The principle of prevention, i.e., the duty to prevent damage, is a general principle controlling the whole field of liability for damages in the Labour Code. The introductory provision of Part 11 of the Labour Code (sections 248 and 249) provides the employer's duty to ensure such working conditions for his employees as will enable them to achieve the proper fulfilment of their working tasks without danger to their health.

337. Also, the whole Part 5 of the Labour Code, concerned with occupational safety and health protection at work, is based on the principle of prevention. Under the provisions of sections 101 and 102 of the Labour Code, the employer is obliged primarily to ensure occupational safety and health protection at work of his employees with reference to risks of possible threats to their lives and health connected with their work performance. The employer is obliged to identify the risks, ascertain their causes and sources and adopt measures for their elimination. For this purpose, he is obliged to check regularly the standard of occupational safety and health protection at work, particularly, the state of technical prevention and the standard of hazard factors of working conditions. Risk prevention is deemed to mean all measures arising from legal and other regulations concerning the assurance of occupational safety and health protection at work and from the employer's measures intended to prevent the risks, to eliminate them or to minimize the effect of those which cannot be eliminated.

338. The employer keeps records of those employees suffering from a certified occupational disease which has originated on the employer's worksites and shall ensure the elimination of such working conditions that generate a risk of the origination of occupational diseases.

339. If there are some risk factors at the employer's worksites, the employer is bound to ascertain and control their values by measurement and ensure their elimination or at least their limitation to the minimum reasonably achievable rate. The number of risk factors includes in particular physical, chemical and biological factors and adverse microclimatic conditions. If the occurrence of biological factors and overstepping of the highest permissible values of risk factors cannot be excluded, the employer is obliged to limit their effect by technical, technological and other measures.

340. Trade union bodies have the right to participate in the ascertainment of the causes of industrial accidents and occupational disease, possibly to investigate them themselves. The employer is bound to ensure the training of the respective trade union bodies and representatives for occupational safety and health protection at work required for the proper performance of their function and make reports and keep records of industrial accidents and recognized occupational diseases available to them.

341. The whole part on health and safety at the workplace was strongly influenced by the relevant directives of the EU law on health and safety.

Chapter 8. Supplementary Benefits

342. There are no supplementary benefits *stricto sensu* for persons affected by an industrial accident or an occupational disease.

343. If an industrial accident results in immobility, there are special immobility benefits regulated by Act No. 329/2011 Coll. on benefits for people with disabilities.

344. Pain and aggravation of social disadvantage due to an industrial accident or occupational disease are not indemnified by a lump-sum any longer, as it used to be until the new Civil Code (Act No. 89/2012 Coll.) entered into force. The Civil Code, among others, abolished the Ordinance No. 440/2001 Coll. on indemnification of pain and aggravation of social assertion, which provided for rules for measuring the damage suffered through pain or aggravation of social assertion (the indemnity was based on a number of points allocated by the physician according to the diagnosis, and the ordinance also defined a value of one point in CZK).

345. The current Civil Code in its section 2958 states: 'When an injury occurred, the pest provides to the victim a reimbursement of the pain suffered, and other non-pecuniary damage. If the injury created an obstacle to better future of the victim, the pest shall compensate also an aggravation of social position of the victim. If the amount of compensation cannot be determined, the principles of fairness shall be applied to determine the amount of compensation.' This vague provision, which is not accompanied by any procedural legislation, is causing some difficulties to the practice, as there are currently no binding rules for determining the amount of damages suffered in any private legal relationship, including damages for a work accident. Such a situation has been criticized and from a practical point of view is not bearable in a long-term perspective.[18] The Supreme Court issued, therefore, a methodology, which is being used for this purpose, which is however not binding and does not have any legal relevance.[19]

18. *See, e.g.*, commentary to the s. 2958 of the Civil Code by J. Vojtek, in Švestka, J., Dvořák, J., Fiala, J. Civil Code – commentary. Wolters Kluwer. Praha, 2014, Doležal, Lavický: Pojetí náhrady nemajetkové újmy při ublížení na zdraví podle nového občanského zákoníku a s tím spojené procesní aspekty. Právní rozhledy 2014, No. 10.
19. Available at http://www.nsoud.cz/JudikaturaNS_new/ns_web.nsf/Metodika.

Chapter 9. No-Fault Insurance

346. This insurance does not come under consideration in the case of industrial accidents because liability for damages due to industrial accidents and occupational diseases is based on the principle of objective responsibility, i.e., responsibility for the result. It is of no consequence whether the employer has or has not caused damage to health or the death of the employee. The employer is obliged to compensate the damage even if he has complied with all obligations arising from legal and other rules concerning the insurance of occupational safety and health protection at work. However, in cases accurately defined by the current legislation, provided the exonerating reasons have been complied with (*see* section 270 of the Labour Code), the employer may be relieved of his liability.

Chapter 10. Civil Liability

347. Liability according to the Labour Code is specific and has such specific rules, as has been shown above, the Civil Code applies in a subsidiary way. General civil liability does not come into consideration as regards liability for industrial accidents or occupational diseases, as the labour legislation is more protective of the employee.

Part VII. Unemployment

Chapter 1. Provision of Work

348. The legislation of the Czech Republic (Act No. 435/2004 Coll.) guarantees the 'right to employment' to all-natural persons (citizens of the Czech Republic or of the other EU Member States or their family members) who want to and are able to work and really seek work. A natural person has a right to select freely her/his employment and perform it in the whole territory of the Czech Republic or abroad.

349. The 'right to employment' is deemed to mean above all:

- the right to the mediation of adequate employment in the Czech Republic;
- the right to retraining necessary for employment;
- the support by means of 'unemployment benefits' before the start of employment and in case of its loss.

350. The 'adequate employment' to the mediation of which the natural person is entitled is deemed to mean such employment:

- which establishes the person's participation in social insurance (and the obligation to pay contributions to the pension insurance to the state employment policy);
- with working hours which make at least 80% of the statutory length of normal working hours;
- which is concluded as 'open-end employment' or as the 'fixed-term employment' with a duration longer than three months;
- corresponds with the person's health status and, if possible, with her/his qualification and skills, the length of her/his previous employment and accommodation possibilities, as well as accessibility by means of transport.

351. In some special cases (e.g., when the person's job applicant status lasts more than one year) the rules of the adequate employment's determination are not so strict.

352. Until the 'adequate employment' is found, the person cannot be excluded (discarded) from the 'register of job applicants' (if no other legal obstacles occur).

§1. Labour (Employment) Mediation

353. The 'employment mediation' is deemed to mean:

(a) seeking employment for a natural person who applies for a job;
(b) seeking employees for an employer who seeks new manpower;
(c) employing of natural persons in order of their work performance for another legal or natural person who gives work to them and supervises their performance (so-called 'user'); this kind of employment mediation is also considered the situation when the foreigner is posted by his foreign employer to work performance in the territory of the Czech Republic on the basis of an agreement with the Czech legal or natural person, whereas the subject matter of the agreement is a 'lease of manpower';
(d) advisory and informational service in the field of work opportunities.

354. The obligation to mediate adequate employment according to the letter (a), (b) and (d) within the whole territory of the Czech Republic has been imposed by the law on the Regional Affiliates of Labour Office of the Czech Republic (hereinafter 'Labour Offices'). This mediation is free of charge.

355. Apart from Labour Offices, employment may also be mediated against payment by other subjects who have granted permission for such activities by the Ministry of Labour and Social Affairs – Employment Agencies). These agencies also perform the activity under the letter (c). By performance of activities under the letters (a), (b) and (d), they cooperate with Labour Offices; they are also entitled to perform these activities on grounds of agreement with Labour Office (so-called shared employment mediation).

356. The natural person may also find adequate employment himself/herself. She/he may turn to any Labour Office with a request for information on free jobs, as all Labour Offices are obliged to advise and inform on free jobs on their files.

357. The Labour Offices provide the 'employment mediation' for two qualified groups of persons – so-called 'job seekers' and 'job applicants'. Besides this, everyone is entitled to get information about employment possibilities or vacancies by any (whichever) Labour Office.

358. The natural person is considered as '**job seeker**' who is interested in mediation if employment and for that purpose she/he (by means of a written application) asks for an enlistment to the 'register of job seekers' by any Labour Office; it is not decisive whether such a person disposes of some employment in time of registration or not. To such persons, the Labour Office mediates adequate employment or it can also ensure retraining for her/him. The 'job seeker' can be excluded from the register if he does not give to the Labour Office necessary cooperation within the process of employment mediation.

359. The natural person is considered as '**job applicant**' who (by means of written application) asks personally the Labour Office (in the municipality of which she/he has got her/his permanent domicile) for mediation of adequate employment and by satisfaction of all statutory conditions she/he is enlisted to the 'register of job applicants'. The conditions are:

- she/he has got her/his permanent domicile in the territory of the Czech Republic;
- she/he is not working in an employment or civil service or any other analogous relationship,
- she/he is not performing any gainful activities as a self-employed person (there are some exceptions to this principle – valid in cases when the range of the gainful activity does not exceed the statutory minimum);
- she/he is not preparing himself/herself for the future profession by studies (with some exceptions);
- she/he is not 'temporarily incapable to work';
- she/he is not imprisoned or in detention or in custody;
- she does not receive 'maternity benefit' in the period of time before the childbirth or in the time of six weeks after the childbirth;
- she/he was not found disabled in the third stage of invalidity (except for persons capable to perform gainful activity by the satisfaction of extraordinary conditions).

360. From 2012, the situation is also considered as the obstacle of the enlistment when:

- the natural person 'without any serious reason' terminates (by himself/herself or on the basis of an agreement with the employer) the adequate employment which was mediated by Labour Office;
- the employer terminates the employment relationship (which was mediated by Labour Office) because the employee has breached some duty, which results from the statutory provisions and relates to her/his work performance, in an especially gross manner.

361. The job applicant registered with a Labour Office is obliged to grant the Office required cooperation and to prove the required facts.

362. Should the job applicant intentionally frustrate the cooperation required for employment mediation or should she/he refuse to enter adequate employment without serious reasons or should any of the above-mentioned obstacles arise during the enlistment, she/he may be (must be) excluded from the register. Such exclusion means serious consequences for her/him – she/he loses the entitlement to the 'unemployment benefit', and she/he loses his/her contribution-free participation in pension insurance as well (*see* below).

363. The 'job applicant' shall be also excluded from the register when she/he asks for such exclusion.

364. In order to help the Labour Office to ensure the 'labour mediation', the employers are enabled to (formerly they were obliged to) notify the Labour Office to the list of free job positions (vacancies) and their characteristics. The Labour Office keeps a register of such vacancies and in case of need it offers these positions to the 'job applicants' or to the 'job seekers'. The employers are also entitled to ask the Labour Office for information about the situation on the labour market or for the advisory service by the draft of appropriate employees from the group of people registered as job applicants.

365. The Employment Act (Act No. 435/2004 Coll.) instructs the Labour Office to grant greater attention to some groups of job applicants who have greater difficulties on the labour market because of their state of health, age, care of a child or other serious reasons.

366. The Labour Office is obliged to work out the so-called individual plan of action for these groups of persons in order to enlarge the chance of their work engagement. The Labour Offices may request the employers to select from the number of reported free jobs those which are suitable for the above-mentioned citizens.

§2. Vocational Training (Retraining)

367. Retraining courses are intended primarily for those 'job applicants' or 'job seekers' who cannot find new employment within their own profession. The retraining can only be provided by so-called *retraining facilities* which means:

- a facility with 'accredited training programme' according to the Employment Act or according to the special regulation; the accreditation can only be awarded or taken away by the Ministry of Education, Youth and Sports;
- universities or other schools with an accredited educational programme;
- the 'retraining facilities' provide the retraining for the 'job seekers' or the 'job applicants' on the basis of an agreement with the Labour Office; in such case, the Labour Office covers the facility's costs of the retraining.

368. The retraining is being realized on the basis of an agreement concluded by the 'job applicant' or the 'job seeker' on one side and the Labour Office on the other side. Although for the natural person, the retraining is free (the costs are fully covered by the Labour Office), the agreement must contain the obligation that the job applicant will refund the Labour Office the retraining costs, should he abandon the training course without serious reasons in the course of its duration or refuse to accept a job corresponding with the acquired qualification on its termination.

369. The retraining courses for employees may also be organized by employers. This retraining is affected in the interest of further employment of the employees in the course of their employment relationship. This retraining is being realized on the basis of an agreement concluded by the employer on one side and the employee on the other side. Besides this, the employer and the Labour Office can conclude an agreement on employee's retraining consisting in gaining, enhancing or extending their education; in such cases, the Labour Office may refund the employer or the retraining facility the expenses of the retraining (fully or partially).

370. This possibility shall not be applied to the cases when the employer is obliged to provide the continuous vocational training to his employees as a precondition for the performance of the work which was concluded in their employment agreement. This only applies to the cases when the retraining concerns the employees who would have to be dismissed because of the fact that their employer changes the object of his enterprise. In these cases, the retraining takes place during the employee's working hours, and they are entitled to wage compensation amounting to their mean earnings in the course of the whole retraining course.

§3. New Job Generating Programmes

371. The Employment Act regulates several other instruments of so-called active employment policy besides the 'retraining'. These instruments are:

- investment incentives;
- community service;
- socially desirable jobs;
- bridging benefit;
- benefit in the season of partial unemployment;
- new-worker-training benefit;
- benefit in case of transition to a new entrepreneurial programme.

372. As an integral part of 'active employment policy' are also considered:

- consultancy given or ensured by the Labour Offices in order to recognize personal and qualifying skills of natural persons for the selection of their occupation, mediation of adequate employment, preparation of handicapped persons for their job and by a selection of an appropriate instrument of active employment policy;
- provisions for support of employment of disabled (handicapped) persons:
  (a) occupational therapy,
  (b) financial support (allowance) for the establishment of a job position for a handicapped person,
  (c) financial support (allowance) for the reimbursement of operating costs paid in connection with the employment of a handicapped person,
  (d) protected labour market,
  (e) allowance for support of employment of handicapped persons within the protected labour market;
- shared mediation of employment (Labour Office in cooperation with private 'employment agency');

– targeted programs for the solution of (un)employment (set of provisions focused on the enhancement of natural 'person's or their 'group's chance to assert themselves on the labour market).

373. The employer to whom a decision about the assurance of 'investment incentive' according to special regulation (Act No. 72/2000 Coll. on investment incentives) was rendered can be entitled to obtain financial support for the purpose of:

– creation of new job opportunities (berths);
– retraining or education of new employees.

374. These benefits are provided by the Labour Office on the basis of the Employment Act only in case that the new berths are created in the territorial area where the rate of unemployment within the two previous half-years (before the submission of employer's intention to gain an investment incentive) is at least 25% higher than the average rate of unemployed persons within the whole Czech Republic or in the area of 'preferential industrial zones' determined by the Government according to a special legislation. The benefits are provided by the Labour Office which concludes an agreement for that purpose with the employer. The agreement must contain the employer's obligation to refund the benefit to the Labour Office in the case that the employer does not draw the financial support in the concluded term. The employer's obligations resulting from the agreement must be fulfilled within three years from the date when the decision on the assurance of investment incentive was issued. The employer who obtained the financial support from the reason of 'investment incentive' is not entitled to be awarded by financial support within any other instrument of the 'active employment policy' for the same purpose.

375. The 'community service' is defined as a time-limited job opportunity for the 'job applicants'. The person's work consists in the public concourses' maintenance, public buildings' or communications' clearance or maintenance or in other similar activities in favour of municipalities, state institutions or other public utility institutions. These works are organized, primarily, for the long-term unemployed or socially disintegrated persons. The duration of such job opportunity is limited to at most twenty-four calendar months; anyway, it can be provided repeatedly. The opportunities are created on the basis of an agreement concluded with the Labour Office; in such a case, the Labour Office has a right to provide the financial support to the employer to a value not exceeding the employer's real expenditures for such employee's remuneration.

376. The job opportunities are considered as 'socially desirable jobs' which were created or reserved by the employer for the 'job applicants' for whom no other job placement can be ensured. The 'socially desirable job' is also such kind of a job opportunity which was created by the 'job applicant' for the purpose of his self-employment's performance. The 'socially desirable job' must always be established on the basis of an agreement concluded with the Labour Office. The person who organizes this kind of job opportunity can be entitled to obtain financial support from the Labour Office for that purpose. The monthly amount of the support is limited (by the number of calendar months or by the multiple of the state average wages), and it is partially dependent on the unemployment rate related to the territorial area where the new job opportunity has been originated.

377. The 'bridging benefit' can be provided by the Labour Office to the self-employed person who ceased to be a 'job applicant' and organized the 'socially desirable jobs' for himself/herself according to the previous paragraph. The sense of the benefit is to help such persons with the operating expenses invested within the transition to the new gainful activity. The benefit is provided on the basis of an agreement concluded with the Labour Office. The monthly amount of the benefit is limited – it makes most highly one-fourth of the state average wages, and it shall be provided for a period of time no longer than five months.

378. The 'benefit in the season of partial unemployment' can be provided by the Labour Office to the employer from the private sector on the basis of an agreement with the employer and after prior consent of the Government. The prerequisite of the entitlement to this benefit is that on the side of such employer occurs an impediment pursuant to the Labour Code consisting in the fact that he is not able to give job to his employees in usual range because of temporary reduction in demand for his products or services provided by him or because of interruption of work caused by a natural disaster, if such employer:

- is unable to give a job to his employees in the range of at least 20% of normal weekly working hours pursuant to the Labour Code;
- already provides to his employees respective wage compensation by reason of such impediment pursuant to the Labour Code and from the day of the agreement's conclusion will provide him with this compensation in the height of at least 70% of the employee's average earnings;
- engages himself in the agreement that within the period concluded for providing the benefit, he will not terminate the employment for organizational reasons with the employee on which the benefit is provided.

The amount of the benefit is limited to 20% of the employee's average earnings, most highly one-eighth of the state average wages, and it shall be provided for a period of time no longer than six months with a possibility of one repetition in the same range.

379. The 'new-worker-training benefit' can be provided by the Labour Office to an employer who receives as an employee a 'job applicant' falling into the group of persons to whom the greater attention on the labour market shall be granted (disabled person, person younger than 20 years of age, etc., *see* above). The benefit is provided on the basis of an agreement concluded between the employer and the Labour Office. The monthly amount of the benefit is limited – it makes most highly one-half of the state minimum wages per one trained person, and it shall be provided for a period of time no longer than three months.

380. The 'benefit in case of transition to a new entrepreneurial programme' can be granted by the Labour Office to an employer who converts to a new entrepreneurial programme and for that reason he is temporarily not able to ensure work for his employees in the full range of 'normal weekly working hours'. The aim of the benefit is to contribute partially to the wage compensation which the employer is obliged to pay to his employees in such cases according to the Labour Code. The benefit is provided on the basis of an agreement concluded between the employer and the Labour Office. The monthly amount of the benefit is limited – it makes most highly one-half of the state minimum wages per employee, and it shall be provided for a period of time no longer than six months.

Chapter 2. Unemployment Benefits

§1. Territorial and Personal Field of Application

381. Unemployment benefits (called 'relief in unemployment' and 'relief in retraining') in the Czech Republic may be granted only to persons with a permanent address in the territory of the Czech Republic if they are:

- citizens of the Czech Republic; or
- family members of the Czech Republic citizens; or
- citizens of the EU and their family members.

382. The benefits cannot be paid abroad, provided that the international treaty, which anchors the obligations of the Czech Republic, incorporated a different provision.

§2. Entitlement Conditions

383. The unemployment benefits shall be granted to persons who are registered by the Labour Office as the 'job applicants'. Their granting, however, is subject to the fulfilment of certain conditions provided by the law (Act No. 435/2004 Coll.). If they have complied with required conditions, all job applicants who have not been mediated adequate employment or assured retraining are entitled to unemployment benefits.

384. The 'relief in unemployment' shall be provided to the 'job applicant' who:

- within the 'decisive period of time' (*two years* before the enlistment to the 'register of job applicants') completed at least *twelve months* of gainful activity which establishes obligatory participation in pension insurance (e.g., employment relationship, service relationship, self-employment, etc. – *see* below);
- asked the Labour Office by which she/he is registered as the 'job applicant' for the award of the 'relief in unemployment';
- to the day from which the 'relief in unemployment' has to be awarded, she/he is not the old-age pension's beneficiary.

385. The necessary gainful activity can be supplied by the so-called *alternative employment period* which is related to persons who cannot perform a gainful activity because they are involved with some social event which does not allow this or because they perform any other activity (of beneficial and unprofitable nature) which takes them the whole time. The Employment Act admits the 'alternative employment period' to these categories of people:

- disabled persons preparing themselves for employment;
- beneficiaries of 'third-range invalidity pension';
- persons taking care of a child up to 4 years of age;

- persons taking personal care of another person who is 'dependent on other person's help' according to the special legislation (Act No. 108/2006 Coll. on Social Services) if such dependent person is in a 'close relation' to her/him or if the dependent person shares a 'common household' with her/him;
- persons who perform a long-term voluntary service on the basis of a contract concluded with the delegating organization (Act No. 198/2002 Coll. on voluntary service);
- persons by who the TIW lasts or were put into quarantine after the termination of a gainful activity which established their participation in sickness insurance if the TIW or quarantine originated during such gainful activity or after its termination in the 'protective period' according to the Act on Sickness Insurance.

386. The person is not entitled to the 'relief in unemployment' who:

- has lost her/his employment within the period of last six months before the enlistment to the 'register of job applicants' by reason that she/he has breached some duty, which results from the statutory provisions and relates to her/his work performance, in an especially gross manner;
- has lost her/his employment within the period of last six months before the enlistment to the 'register of job applicants' by reason that she/he has breached some duty related to their 'temporary-incapacity-to-work regime' in an especially gross manner;
- is entitled to receive a 'serve-out benefit' according to special regulations whereas the amount of the benefit is higher than the amount of the potential 'relief in unemployment';
- performs a gainful activity which does not obstruct to the enlistment in the register of job applicants (the employment with remuneration not higher than a half of the state minimum wage).

387. To the 'job applicant' who has fulfilled the statutory conditions, the 'relief in unemployment' belongs from the day of the application for the benefit. If the application is submitted no later than three working days after the termination of a gainful activity or of one of the above-mentioned alternative employment periods, the 'relief in unemployment' shall be awarded from the day which follows the day of such termination. The 'job applicant' is also obliged to submit to the Labour Office documentary proofs of all decisive facts.

388. The 'relief in retraining' shall be provided to the 'job applicant' who participates in the retraining ensured by the Labour Office and to the day from which the 'relief in retraining' has to be awarded she/he is not the old-age pension's beneficiary. This benefit can be provided for the whole time the retraining lasts.

389. If the natural person is not entitled to unemployment benefits, has no other source of income and is socially needy, she/he shall be granted 'social care benefits' (*see* below).

§3. PERIOD OF BENEFIT PAYMENT

390. The job applicant is entitled to 'relief in unemployment' most highly for the maximum 'period of support' which makes:

- five months during her/his age up to 50;
- eight months during her/his age between 50 and 55 years;
- eleven months during her/his age over 55 years.

391. The 'decisive age' is considered the age at the time when the application was submitted.

392. If the natural person starts working after the elapse of the 'period of support' whereas her/his employment lasts at least six months and she/he, subsequently, becomes unemployed again, she/he shall be entitled to 'relief in unemployment' again for the whole 'period of support'.

393. Under certain circumstances, however, the 'relief in unemployment' is not granted even if the natural person has complied with the required conditions. This happens in cases when the material security of the person during her/his unemployment is assured by other sources, e.g., if she/he complies with entitlement conditions of 'old-age pension', if he receives sickness insurance benefits replacing wages or has started custody or imprisonment. The gaining of unemployment benefit is also blocked-up if the beneficiary begins to perform a gainful activity which does not obstruct to the enlistment in the register of job applicants (the employment with remuneration not higher than a half of the state minimum wage). If the 'job applicant' is entitled to receive a lump-sum from his ex-employer as compensation of his redundancy, the 'relief in unemployment' shall not be provided for a period of time which corresponds to the number of months from which the amount of the lump-sum was determined.

394. The entitlement to the 'relief in unemployment' lapses when:

- the period of support expires;
- the enlistment of a person in the 'register of job applicants' is terminated;
- the person is excluded from the 'register of job applicants'.

If the 'period of support' has elapsed and the natural person is no longer entitled to 'relief in unemployment' and is socially needy (in material distress), she/he shall be granted 'social care benefits'.

§4. AMOUNT OF THE BENEFIT

395. The amount of unemployment benefits is based on the mean net monthly earnings achieved by the natural person in her/his last employment. If the job applicant's last gainful activity was self-employment, the amount of the benefits is based on the net monthly pension insurance calculation base used in the 'decisive period of time'.

396. In the case of the 'relief in unemployment', the amount is dependent on the time-length of the individual's unemployment and is determined at the rate of:

- 65% of these earnings within the first two months of unemployment;
- 50% of these earnings within the further two months of unemployment;
- 45% of these earnings within the rest of the period of support.

397. In the case that the 'job applicant' has terminated his job without any 'serious statutory reason', the amount of his benefit makes 45% of these earnings within the whole 'period of support'.

398. In the matter of the 'relief in retraining', the amount of the benefit makes 60% of the above-mentioned earnings, and it is provided for the whole duration of the retraining course.

399. If the 'job applicant' cannot prove the amount of her/his income through no fault of her/his own or if within the 'decisive period of time', she/he has completed only 'alternative employment periods', the amount of her/his unemployment benefits is calculated from the 'average state wages' (CZK 28,761 valid for 2016). In the case of:

(a) 'relief in unemployment' it makes:
   - 0.15-multiple of the average state wages within the first two months of unemployment (CZK 4,315 valid for 2018);
   - 0.12-multiple of the average state wages within the further two months of unemployment (CZK 3,452 valid for 2018);
   - 0.11-multiple of the average state wages within the rest of the period of support (CZK 3,164 valid for 2018).

(b) 'relief in retraining' – it makes 0.14-multiple of the average state wages within the whole duration of the retraining course (CZK 4,027 valid for 2018).

400. The *maximum amount of unemployment benefits* is also determined by means of the 'average state wages'. In the case of:

- 'relief in unemployment' – it makes *0.58-multiple* of the average state wages (CZK 16,682 valid for 2018);
- 'relief in retraining' – it makes *0.65-multiple* of the average state wages (CZK 18,695 valid for 2018).

§5. Benefit Procedure

401. Any job applicant who has complied with statutory conditions is legally entitled to unemployment benefits. The Labour Office certifies this entitlement by its decision on their payment. The decision on benefit payment is issued as a result of administrative procedure and is subject to appeal.

402. If the decision on the appeal is not made by the Labour Office, which has issued the original decision, the appeal is decided by the Ministry of Labour and Social Affairs. On the termination of the appellate procedure, it is possible to request the judicial review of the legally effective decision of the appellate authority by a Regional Court.

403. The Labour Office decision on benefit payment is based on the data provided by the job applicant. If the benefits were granted and paid unlawfully or at a higher rate than actually due through the job applicant's fault, he is obliged to refund the unlawfully paid amount to the Labour Office. However, the refunding title expires after the elapse of five years from the day of their granting.

404. The job applicant is also obliged to refund the benefits or a part thereof if his action concerning the termination of employment relationship is decided by the court in his favour, declaring the termination void and making the employer pay her/him a wage compensation for the period in which the employer did not assign her/him any work. The benefit refund is also required if it has been ascertained, subsequently, that the job applicant has complied with the conditions of 'old-age pension' or of the 'third-stage pensions'.

Part VIII. Pensions

405. This part deals with the system of pension insurance of wage-earners, further groups of people performing work or analogous activities and self-employment. If the insured persons comply with statutory conditions, they are all granted the same type of pension insurance benefits in case of old age, invalidity and breadwinner's death.

406. Apart from state-guaranteed pension benefits, there is also the possibility of private 'supplementary insurance' with state contribution operated by pension funds/pension companies.

407. As mentioned above, the history of the Czech pension insurance is being written since 1996 when Act No. 155/1995 Coll. on pension insurance became effective. During the twenty years of its effectivity, the legal regulation has been amended more than fifty times! On one side, this fact shows evidence of dynamic evolvement of this branch of the law of its ability to react flexibly on public demand. On the other side, it points to its extraordinary dependence on the political and economic situation and of responsible persons' inability to think and work in favour of this regulation's stability and apprehensibility, especially for ordinary people who are the primary recipients of its content.

408. Hereto, we can name the most important amendments from the recent period.

409. Act No. 24/2006 Coll. (effective from 1 February 2006) which derogated the so-called economic condition for the entitlement to payment of invalidity pension – till that date an income from parallel gainful activity (in specified statutory amount) was considered as an obstacle of invalidity pension payment.

410. Act No. 306/2008 Coll. (effective from 1 January 2010) brought important 'parametric changes' to the system of pension insurance. The purpose of these changes was a priori to 'toughen up' the conditions of entitlement to old-age pension (longer minimum length of the necessary insurance period, higher 'retirement age') as a means of a solution for the problems related to the unfavourable demographic evolvement. This Act also brought some simplifications, e.g., the two separate kinds of invalidity pensions ('partial invalidity pension' and 'full invalidity pension') were replaced by unique benefit (invalidity pension) provided in three different amounts according to the certified stage of invalidity.

411. Act No. 220/2011 Coll. (effective since 30 September 2011, partially from 1 January 2012) brought important changes in the pattern of calculation on pensions – under the specific Decision of Constitutional Court of the Czech Republic (No. 135/2010 Coll.) the principle of merit (equivalency) should be empowered so the people with higher incomes should enjoy higher pensions in the future (the less wealthy people, on the contrary, will enjoy lower pensions). From January 2012, the statutory measures for the reduction of 'early old-age pension' are less favourable. Even the conditions of the entitlement to the widow's and widower's pension are lightly modified.

412. Act No. 470/2011 Coll. (effective from 1 January 2012) brought some new specific categories of insured persons (members of legal persons' collective bodies, holders of procuration, company liquidators and others) and again established a tight link between the participation on sickness and pension insurance. The conditions of the entitlement to the orphan's pension are lightly modified in favour of the orphaned children.

413. Act No. 303/2013 Coll. and the Legal measure of the Senate No. 344/2013 Coll. (both effective from 1 January 2014) brought some partial changes in connection with the total re-codification of private law in the Czech legal order – new Civil Code No. 89/2012 Coll. and Act No. 90/2012 Coll. on Business Corporations (that became effective to the same date). For example, they brought a new category of insured persons – 'persons delegated to perform trade management pursuant to contractual representation' or they transferred the definition of 'common household' from Civil Code to the Act on Pension Insurance.

414. Act No. 267/2014 Coll. (effective from 1 January 2015) brought a new type of old-age pension in order to ensure compliance of the Czech legal order with the Article 18 paragraph 2 subparagraph (a) of the International Labour Organization Convention No. 128 – Invalidity, Old-Age and Survivors' Benefits Convention (*see* below).

415. Act No. 213/2016 Coll. (effective from 1 October 2016) brought some important changes within the conditions of entitlement to the old-age pension for mineworkers as a special category of workers (very hard-working persons who deserve special treatment – *see* below).

416. Act No. 203/2017 Coll. (effective from 1 August 2017, partially from 1 January 2018) brought important changes within the rules for determining the 'retirement age'. According to the previous legislation, the *maximal limit of retirement age was not laid down.* Now the upper limit of the retirement age has settled down to 65 years. At the same time, the Government is obliged to revise (evaluate) the regulation of the retirement age every five years with regard to the demographic movement; in accordance with the results of such analyses, the upper limit of the retirement age should be moved up or down.

417. Act No. 259/2017 Coll. (effective from 1 February 2018) brought several less-important changes taking into account experience in the application of pension regulation in practice.

418. Act No. 191/2018 Coll. (effective since 1 September 2018, partially from 1 January 2019) brings important changes into the sphere of the amount of benefits (pensions). This act lays down that since 2019, the amount of the 'basic part' of all pensions shall increase from 9% of average wages to 10% of average wages; in 2019, the amount makes CZK 3,270. The other change is that the pensions belonging to people who have reached 85 years of age shall increase to CZK 1,000.

Chapter 1. Pensions for Wage-Earners

419. Under Act No. 155/1995 Coll. on Pension Insurance, the wage-earners ('employees' in Czech legislation), like other persons performing work or similar activities, are entitled to old-age, invalidity, widow's or widower's and orphan's pension. In theory and practice, these pensions are divided into direct and indirect (derived) pensions. The differentiation criterion is, whether they are based on direct entitlement of the beneficiary from her/his pension insurance (old-age and invalidity pensions) or whether such person derives her/his entitlement from another person's entitlement (survivors' pensions).

420. Apart from citizens of the Czech Republic, the same entitlement to pension (old-age, invalidity or survivors' pension) has, since 1 May 2004, also applied to citizens of the EU (and their family members), provided that they have been insured for at least one year and satisfy the other defined conditions (e.g., they reached the retirement age). They will get their pension paid without any changes or reduction. For the purposes of the acquisition of the right to benefit from the Czech pension system, all the insurance periods completed in individual Member States of the EU shall be considered together. The amount of benefit paid is then determined in accordance with the ratio of the duration of the periods of insurance before the rise of the respective social event under the legislation which it administers to the total duration of the periods of insurance completed before the rise of the respective social event under the legislations of all the Member States concerned (so-called sub-pension).

421. Similar rules are also applied to citizens of many other states (outside the EU) which the Czech Republic has concluded the Treaty on Social Security with.

422. The Pension Insurance Act enables the valorization of all paid pensions in relation to the increase of 'consumer prices' and to the evolvement of 'state average wages'. The paid pensions are valorized by an Order of the Government (from 2012 to 2015 by an Ordinance of Ministry of Labour and Social Affairs) regularly each January, namely in dependence on the amount of the increase of these indexes. The pensions must be valorized in 'extraordinary term', provided that the increase in prices since the last pension valorization has reached at least 5%. From 2016, the Government is entitled to decide on 'higher than necessary' valorization up to 2.7% of the value of 'state average old-age pension'.

§1. Old-Age Pension

423. The 'old-age pensions' are intended to ensure the compensation of unfavourable consequences of a social event called 'old age'. The 'old age' is represented by the 'retirement age' which can be defined as an age declared by the state and laid down by law which is considered as an objective beginning of each person's incapacity to work caused by the exhaustion of the human organism.

424. The 'parametric changes' (effective since 2010) brought many changes to this branch of law. The most important of them are described below.

I. Beneficiaries

A. Territorial Field of Application

425. It is possible to say that the receipt of pension benefits from the Czech pension insurance system is not bound to the territory of the Czech Republic. All Czech citizens living in the territory of the Czech Republic, citizens of the EU, as well as the persons living permanently abroad are *entitled to an old-age pension* if they have complied with statutory conditions.

426. They are also entitled to *receive payment of the pension* in the country of their living. The only condition necessary to satisfy for the payment of benefit abroad is to submit the so-called 'certificate of living' at least once per calendar year. The CSSA automatically sends this certificate to the address of a pensioner in the respective foreign country every calendar year. The period of return of the filled-in form signed by a beneficiary is thirty calendar days from the day of its delivery. When the CSSA receives back the confirmed form, it shall send the payment to the beneficiary. All payment transfers are made through the Czech National Bank in Prague and its contractual partners – its correspondent banks.

427. As regards the obligatory participation of employees in the pension insurance, the territorial criteria is identical to the territorial criteria of the obligatory participation of employees in the sickness insurance (performance of the employment in the territory of the Czech Republic, performance of the employment abroad for the employer whose registered place of business is in the territory of the Czech Republic, etc.). However, the Czech legislation also allows voluntary participation (of employees or other persons) in pension insurance which is fully freed from the link to the territory of the Czech Republic.

428. In the cases of payment of the respective pension abroad, with the exception of Member States of the European Economic Community, it is important to differentiate whether a social security agreement has been concluded with the respective state, which makes it possible to pay the pension to the territory of another state, when the beneficiary lives there permanently.

B. Personal Field of Application

429. The prerequisite of entitlement, which is common for all of the pension benefits, is to complete the amount of insurance period which corresponds, at least, to the statutory minimum of the 'necessary insurance period'. The determination as to who is insured and who is not is whereas very important. The Act on pension insurance regulates (differentiates) three ways of participation in insurance.

1. By Reason of Gainful Activity

430. The range of insured persons (employees) and the conditions of their participation are identical to the rules applied in the field of sickness insurance – the participation in these two systems of insurance is tightly linked. The participation in pension insurance is, therefore, obligatory for:

- Workers with an employment relationship.
- Officers of the Police of Czech Republic, the Fire Rescue Service of Czech Republic, the Customs Administration of Czech Republic, the Prison Service of Czech Republic, the General Inspection of Security Brigades, the Security Information Service, the Office for Foreign Relations and Information, professional soldiers and soldiers with an inactive status at the time when they perform active military service.
- Civil servants under the Act on Civil Service.
- Members of cooperatives who, outside the contractual employment relationship, perform work for the cooperative for which they are remunerated by the cooperative.
- Employees performing their gainful activity on the basis of 'Agreements on Working Activity' or 'Agreement on Work Performance' (special labour law relationships different from the main employment relationship).
- Workers with an employment relationship established under foreign legislation.
- Judges.
- Members of the Boards of Representatives of territorial self-governing units and Boards of Representatives of municipal quarters or municipal districts of territorially divided statutory cities and the Capital of Prague who have been elected to functions which were determined by the Boards of Representatives as functions for which the Members of the Boards of Representatives must be disengaged from their regular occupations.
- Members of the Lower House of Parliament and Senators of the Senate of the Czech Parliament.
- Members of the government, President, Vice-President and Members of the Supreme Audit Office, Members of the Council for Radio and Television Broadcasting, Members of the Board of the Office for Energetic Regulation, Members of the Board of the Institute for Studying Totalitarian Regimes, Members of the National Budget Council, Members of the Board of the Czech Telecommunication Office, Financial Arbitrator and Deputy Financial Arbitrator, Public Defender of Rights and Deputy Public Defender of Rights.
- Natural entities who, under special law, are appointed or elected chiefs of an administrative authority or a statutory body of a legal entity established under special law, or a deputy for this chief or statutory body if this chief or statutory body is just one entity and the appointment or election did not result in establishing an employment or service relationship for these persons; natural entities who, under special law, discharge a public function outside an employment or service relationship if their employment relationship is subject to the specified scope of the Labour Code.
- Voluntary home care services staff.

- Foster parents working in facilities designed for this purpose under special legislation, or who are paid remuneration for foster care that foster parents are paid in special events and under special legislation.
- Imprisoned convicts involved in a work process.
- People working under a relationship with the same content as an employment relationship, but without establishing the employment relationship because the conditions set out by labour law for establishing an employment relationship are not met.
- Partners and executives of limited liability companies and limited partners in special limited partnerships if they carry out work for the company outside of an employment relationship, and directors of not-for-profit organizations if they carry out work for the company outside of an employment relationship.
- Authorized agents (proxies).
- Members of collective bodies of legal persons.
- Liquidators (receivers).
- Directors of branches of legal persons whose place of work is permanently situated in the Czech Republic.
- Persons delegated to perform trade management pursuant to contractual representation.
- Persons not mentioned in previous points.

All these groups of persons are a party to pension insurance when they perform an 'occupation', that means a gainful activity if the incomes of such activity are or could be deemed incomes from dependent activity under the Income Tax Act and are not free of this tax.

431. There are also special rules of participation applicable in the situation when, in spite of the legal existence of the employment, the real work is not performed because of some legal or factual obstacle. Under these circumstances, the participation in insurance lasts only if in the respective calendar month at least one of these conditions is satisfied:

- any income was accounted;
- the employee performed his work for at least one day within the calendar month;
- existence of the so-called excusatory reason (e.g., TIW) for at least one day within the calendar month.

432. If none of these conditions is satisfied, such calendar month cannot be considered as insured. These rules are not applied by some special kinds of gainful activity ('Agreement on Work Performance', 'short-range employment') by which the participation in insurance is only conditioned by minimum accounted income (statutory amount).

2. By Reason of So-Called Alternative Insurance Period

433. This possibility appertains to a relatively wide range of people who cannot perform a gainful activity because they are involved with some social event which does not allow this or because they perform any other activity (of beneficial and unprofitable nature) which keeps them occupied the whole time. The following groups of people fall within this category:

- persons registered by Labour Offices as job applicants – the period entitling them to enjoy unemployment benefits is considered every time, the period in which they are not entitled to enjoy unemployment benefits is considered, maximally, for three years within their whole life (and prior to the fifty-fifth year of age, maximally, for one year);
- disabled persons preparing themselves for employment;
- persons taking care of a child up to 4 years of age;
- persons taking personal care of another person who is deemed 'dependent on other person's help' according to the special legislation (Act No. 108/2006 Coll. on Social Services) if such dependent person is in a 'close relation' to her/him or if the dependent person shares a 'common household' with her/him or if the person who provides the care is in position of 'social-care assistant';
- beneficiaries of 'third-range invalidity pension' who have not attained the age limit required for the entitlement to old-age pension (retirement age);
- persons receiving sickness benefits after the termination of a gainful activity;
- persons who are subject to special witness protection programme if they cannot perform any gainful activity;
- persons who prepared themselves for future professions by studies at a medium-grade or high-grade school (for six years after the age of 18 years) before 2010;
- persons who performed compulsory military service as a civilian service before 2005 or as a service in the army before July 2016 (but were not in the position of professional soldiers).

434. The 'alternative insurance period' can only be considered if their gainer has completed at least one year of the 'standard insurance period' (i.e., the insurance period by reason of gainful activity) within the whole of her/his life.

435. The consideration of these 'alternative insurance periods' is the same, in principle, as the consideration of insurance periods completed by reason of gainful activity (only in some cases the length of these periods is being reduced to 80% for purposes of the entitlement to the benefits or only for the amount of them). This is an expression of an outstanding social accent in the Czech pension system which is, however, very burdening for the state budget (especially in times of economic crises).

3. Voluntary Participation

436. The voluntary participation in pension insurance can be appropriate for persons over 18 years of age who do not satisfy the above-mentioned conditions of obligatory participation (they are not insured *ex lege*) whereas they want to be insured (and pay the contributions at minimum amount CZK 2,289 per month – valid for 2019) in order to gain entitlement to pension benefit in the future. The Act on pension insurance differentiates the participation from some of the 'qualified reasons' (the conditions of participation are more favourable) and the participation 'without reason'.

437. It is possible to participate in voluntary pension insurance for the *following reasons*:

(a) an individual is registered by Labour Office as a 'job applicant' whereas the unemployment benefits or retraining benefits are not awarded for this period;
(b) systematic preparation for a future occupation – secondary school, college or university in the Czech Republic (or abroad if – according to the decision of the Ministry of Education – such study programme is equal to study programmes at secondary schools and universities in the Czech Republic);
(c) gainful activity abroad after 31 December 1995;
(d) long-term voluntary service on the basis of a contract concluded with the delegating organization (in force from 1 January 2003);
(e) activity in the Czech Republic on behalf of so-called 'foreign employer' in the case of individuals, who are employed by a foreign employer and who act in favour of this employer in the Czech Republic (in force from 1 January 2009);
(f) discharge of the office of Deputy of European Parliament elected in the territory of the Czech Republic (in force from 19 September 2009);
(g) residence abroad for the reason of accompanying one's spouse who works as a member of the diplomatic corps of the Czech Republic (in force from 1 January 2010, amended from 1 January 2015).

438. The voluntary participation in insurance under letters (a) and (b) can be applied retroactively prior to submission of the application without any time limits (at most to the date 1 January 1996), (c), (d) and (e) can also be applied retroactively prior to submission of the application, however, no longer than two years immediately preceding the day of submission, (f) and (g) can be applied retroactively prior to submission of the application without any time limits (however, at most to the date of effectivity of the respective statutory amendment – 19 September 2009, 1 January 2010, resp. 1 January 2015).

439. It is also possible to participate in voluntary pension insurance *without the existence of any of the statutory qualified reasons.* In such case, however, the participation is possible to the maximum limit of ten years within the whole person's life. This participation can be applied retroactively prior to submission of the application, however, no longer than one year immediately preceding the day of submission. From 1 February 2018, this kind of voluntary participation in pension insurance is possible only for persons who gained, at least, 1 year of obligatory participation (gainful activity) before the day of giving application to voluntary participation.

440. From 1 January 2012, the participation in voluntary pension insurance is possible only until the day that immediately anticipates the day of acquisition of the entitlement to an old-age pension.

441. The applications to the voluntary participation on pension insurance shall be submitted to the respective DSSA. This authority also carries on the related agenda.

II. Conditions

A. *Old-Age Pensions at Retirement Age ('Regular' Old-Age Pension)*

442. There are two fundamental entitlement conditions:

– gain of the 'required insurance period';
– reach of the 'retirement age'.

443. As mentioned above, from 2010 within the so-called parametrical changes the 'required insurance period' is being gradually extended, namely, from primary twenty-five years to final thirty-five years. For determination of the 'required period of insurance' by the concrete individual, only the calendar year when she/he reaches the retirement age is decisive. The length of the 'required period of insurance' necessary for a gain of the entitlement to the old-age pension is stated in the following table:

The Calendar Year of the Retirement Age	*Required Period of Insurance*
before 2010	25 years
in 2010	26 years
in 2011	27 years
in 2012	28 years
in 2013	29 years
in 2014	30 years
in 2015	31 years
in 2016	32 years
in 2017	33 years
in 2018	34 years
after 2018	35 years

444. The insured individuals who have not completed the required period of insurance to the day of reaching 'retirement age' shall not be entitled to receive an old-age pension from such date. Their entitlement will arise after the completion of the necessary minimum amount of the required period of insurance (derived, however, from the year of the retirement age).

445. Whereas the fact that the above-mentioned periods can be considered by many people as too long, the respective legislation lays down even an alternative condition insisting in gaining the period of insurance in the range of just thirty years (valid for persons who reached the retirement age in 2015 and later). However, this range is sufficient only in the case that it was 'contributory participation', that means connected with an obligation to pay the contributions to the pension system (employment, self-employment, voluntary participation – but not the alternative insurance periods).

446. As regards the 'retirement age', this one is also being increased gradually. Moreover, it is still differentiated according to the year of birth, gender and number of brought-up children (by women). Until 31 December 1995, the required retirement age was 60 years for men and 53–57 years for women (57 years, if they have not brought-up any children, 56 years in case of one, 55 years in case of two, 54 years in case of three or four and 53 years in case of five and more brought-up children). These age limits are still valid for people born prior to 1936.

447. The 'retirement age' of persons who were born after 1935 is stated in the table below:

Year of Birth	*Men*	*Women (According to the Number of Brought-up Children)*				
Childless	*1 Child*	*2 Children*	*3 or 4 Children*	*5 and More Children*		
Prior to 1936	60	57	56	55	54	53
1936	60*) + 2**)	57	56	55	54	53
1937	60 + 4	57	56	55	54	53
1938	60 + 6	57	56	55	54	53
1939	60 + 8	57 + 4	56	55	54	53
1940	60 + 10	57 + 8	56+ 4	55	54	53
1941	61	58	56 + 8	55 + 4	54	53
1942	61 + 2	58 + 4	57	55 + 8	54 + 4	53

Year of Birth	*Men*	*Women (According to the Number of Brought-up Children)*				
Childless	*1 Child*	*2 Children*	*3 or 4 Children*	*5 and More Children*		
1943	61 + 4	58 + 8	57 + 4	56	54 + 8	53 + 4
1944	61 + 6	59	57 + 8	56 + 4	55	53 + 8
1945	61 + 8	59 + 4	58	56 + 8	55 + 4	54
1946	61 + 10	59 + 8	58 + 4	57	55 + 8	54 + 4
1947	62	60	58 + 8	57 + 4	56	54 + 8
1948	62 + 2	60 + 4	59	57 + 8	56 + 4	55
1949	62 + 4	60 + 8	59 + 4	58	56 + 8	55 +4
1950	62 + 6	61	59 + 8	58 + 4	57	55 + 8
1951	62 + 8	61 + 4	60	58 + 8	57 + 4	56
1952	62 + 10	61 + 8	60 + 4	59	57 + 8	56 + 4
1953	63	62	60 + 8	59 + 4	58	56 + 8
1954	63 + 2	62 + 4	61	59 + 8	58 + 4	57
1955	63 + 4	62 + 8	61 + 4	60	58 + 8	57 + 4
1956	63 + 6	63 + 2	61 + 8	60 + 4	59	57 + 8
1957	63 + 8	63 + 8	62 + 2	60 + 8	59 + 4	58
1958	63 + 10	63 + 10	62 + 8	61 + 2	59 + 8	58 + 4
1959	64	64	63 + 2	61 + 8	60 + 2	58 + 8
1960	64 + 2	64 + 2	63 + 8	62 + 2	60 + 8	59 + 2

Year of Birth	*Men*	*Women (According to the Number of Brought-up Children)*				
Childless	*1 Child*	*2 Children*	*3 or 4 Children*	*5 and More Children*		
1961	64 + 4	64 + 4	64 + 2	62 + 8	61 + 2	59 + 8
1962	64 + 6	64 + 6	64 + 6	63 + 2	61 + 8	60 + 2
1963	64 + 8	64 + 8	64 + 8	63 + 8	62 + 2	60 + 8
1964	64 + 10	64 + 10	64 + 10	64 + 2	62 + 8	61 + 2
1965	65	65	65	64 + 8	63 + 2	61 + 8
1966	65	65	65	65	63 + 8	62 + 2
1967	65	65	65	65	64 + 2	62 + 8
1968	65	65	65	65	64 + 8	63 + 2
1969	65	65	65	65	65	63 + 8
1970	65	65	65	65	65	64 + 2
1971	65	65	65	65	65	64 + 8

Notes: *) years, **) months.

448. For persons born after 1971 the 'retirement age' is stipulated at 65 years. This rule, however, could change in the near future. From 2018, the Government shall revise (evaluate) the regulation of the retirement age every five years with regard to the demographic movement and in accordance with the results of respective analyses the Government is meant to propose correction of the present regulation of 'retirement age' (move the upper limit up or down).

449. Within its interim provisions, the Act on pension insurance also regulates rules for determination of 'retirement age' for special groups of persons who:

– performed so-called first-category employment (extremely hard works like mineworkers, mining engineers, airmen, etc.) before 1993; however, the respective legislation from recent times (Order of the Government No. 363/2009 Coll., Act No. 213/2016 Coll.) also deals with special rules of the retirement age of mineworkers who performed this activity even after 1992 – e.g. according to the Act No. 213/2016 Coll. their retirement age is seven years lower than the general retirement age if they had performed this activity for at least 3,300 work shifts;

– were members of the resistance (especially World War II); for these individuals, the lower retirement age limit laid down by regulations effective prior to 1 January 1996 remains valid.

450. The condition of child upbringing (her own, adopted or accepted for permanent care) is deemed to have been complied with if the woman personally takes care of the child until her/his majority for at least ten years. If she has started her/his upbringing after the child has reached 8 years of age, the condition of personal care is satisfied if the care lasts for at least five years.

451. The individual who satisfies both conditions of entitlement is not obliged to submit a claim for an award of pension from the retirement-age-day. Such person has a possibility to continue in the gainful activity and then submit a claim for an award of pension from the retirement-age-day (i.e., retroactively) or from some later date – the choice of a later day will lead to a higher amount of the pension.

B. 'Proportional' Old-Age Pension

452. Both men and women who do not succeed to gain the 'requested period of insurance' for the 'regular old-age pension' neither to the date of the retirement age nor to the later age have a possibility to gain the entitlement by satisfying special conditions insisting in a shorter period of insurance but higher required age. Even these conditions are being 'toughened up' gradually from 2010. The newly laid down age, as well as the new amounts of the 'requested period of insurance' are stated in the following table:

Required Age (Valid for Men and Women) in the Calendar Year	*Requested Insurance Period*
65 years *before* 2010	15 years
retirement age of a man born on the same date + 5 years in 2011	17 years
retirement age of a man born on the same date + 5 years in 2012	18 years
retirement age of a man born on the same date + 5 years in 2013	19 years
retirement age of a man born on the same date + 5 years after 2013	20 years

However, such conditions were subsequently found non-complying with Article 18 paragraph 2 subparagraph (a) of the International Labour Organization Convention No. 128 ('Where the old-age benefit is conditional upon a minimum period of contribution or employment, a reduced benefit shall be secured at least to a person protected who has completed, prior to the contingency, in accordance with prescribed rules, a qualifying period of 15 years of contribution or employment.').

That's why the above-mentioned Act No. 267/2014 Coll. (effective from 1 January 2015) brought an amendment, which enables to gain entitlement to 'proportional old-age pension' also in the case that the persons who reach the required age after 2010 have gathered the insurance period in the range of fifteen years. This range is only sufficient in case that it was 'contributory participation' (employment, self-employment, voluntary participation – but not the 'alternative insurance periods').

C. Old-Age Pensions Before Retirement Age Permanently Reduced ('Early' Old-Age Pension)

453. Apart from the above-mentioned classical old-age benefits, the legislation in force in the Czech Republic makes it possible to obtain old-age pension before the reach of retirement age. The purpose of this old-age pension is to enable earlier retirement to those who decide to do so at their own free will and have acquiesced with the permanently negative impact of this decision on the amount of the benefits. Once this type of old-age pension is granted, it excludes any further entitlement to 'regular old-age pension'.

454. For the entitlement to the 'early' old-age pension, the following conditions must be satisfied:

(1) gain of the 'required insurance period' which is the same as by the entitlement to the 'regular old-age pension' – to the date of origin of the entitlement to the 'early' old-age pension the person must have already gained the 'required insurance period' necessary for 'regular old-age pension' (i.e., derived from the year of the real retirement age);
(2) reach of the required age which is also derived from 'retirement age' and makes:
   - at most three years prior to the 'retirement age' if the real retirement age makes less than 63 years;
   - 60 years if the 'retirement age' makes at least 63 years;
   - at most five years prior to the 'retirement age' if the real retirement age makes more than 65 years (will be used in the future).

455. The entitlement to the 'early' old-age pension can be admitted earliest to the day of submission of the claim – retroactive admission is impossible. The day of admission of this pension is considered as the day of the origin of the entitlement.

456. The precocity of granting of this pension is compensated by its so-called precocity reduction which becomes higher as the period of precocity becomes longer. The nature of this reduction is permanent, i.e., after the admission, the reduction cannot be pulled down (except in the situation when the payment of benefit must have been suspended by reason of resumption of gainful activity).

457. The previous regulation also provided so-called ‘temporarily reduced’ old-age pension before retirement age. This benefit used to be recalculated to the day of retirement age – the ‘precocity reduction’ was pulled down and the pension was thenceforward as high as the regular old-age pension. This benefit, however, was abolished by Act No. 306/2008 Coll. because the conditions of this benefit did not correspond to the principles of social insurance.

III. Calculation of an Old-Age Pension

458. The ‘old-age’ pension is structured as a two-component benefit, consisting of the basic and the percentage components.

459. The ‘basic component’ is identical for all pension types and from 2012 makes 9% of the ‘state average wages’; from the year 2019 the amount of this component shall make 10 % of the ‘state average wages’. Its accurate amount shall be declared to the public through an Order of the Government; at present (the year 2018), it amounts to CZK 2,700 per month, in the year 2019 it shall amount to CZK 3,270 per month.

460. The ‘percentage component’ is determined as a percentage of calculation base derived from the beneficiaries’ average monthly gross incomes – these real average incomes are reduced by means of ‘reduction levels’ in order to apply the solidarity of wealthy people to the poor ones; as a reaction to the Constitutional Court’s decision, the reduction rules were changing gradually every calendar year (during 2011–2015) in order to empower the ‘equivalence principle’ at the expense of the ‘solidarity principle’. The percentage rate consists of the rate regarding insurance period gained before the origin of entitlement and after this origin. The legislation enables an increase of the percentage component, if the insured person who has complied with entitlement conditions does not draw the old-age pension and continues to work. The percentage rate for the insurance period before the entitlement date amounts to 1.5% of the calculation base for every year of the insurance period. For the persons who were a party to the pension savings (according to Act No. 426/2011 Coll. on pension savings effective in 2013–2015) and who did not refund the brought-out premium back to the state budget till the end of the year 2017 the percentage rate for the insurance period before the entitlement date amounts to 1.2% of the calculation base for every year of the parallel participation in the pension insurance and the pension savings. The percentage rate for the period of gainful activities performed after the entitlement date amounts to 1.5% of the calculation base for every entire period of ninety calendar days of gainful activity. The pension component arising from these percentage rates amounts minimally to CZK 770 per month.

461. From 2010, the legislation also enables to increase the percentage component of the pension by consideration of an insurance period gained during the pension’s payment. The increase is not as favourable as if the benefit is not granted –

its amount makes 0.4% of the calculation base for every entire period of 360 calendar days of such gainful activity. Similar principle is applied also when the beneficiary only claims the payment of one-half of the benefit – the increase makes 1.5% of the calculation base for every entire period of 180 calendar days of such gainful activity.

462. The amount of the 'early' old-age pension also consists of the basic and the percentage components. The amount of the basic component is the same as in the preceding case (CZK 2,700 in 2018 and CZK 3,270 in 2019). The percentage component is calculated in the same way except that the amount of the percentage rate is reduced by reason of the precocity as follows:

- 0.9% of the calculation base per each even initiated period of 90 calendar days within the period of the first 360 calendar days of precocity;
- 1.2% of the calculation base per each even initiated period of 90 calendar days within the period from the 361st calendar day to 720th calendar day of precocity;
- 1.5% of the calculation base per each even initiated period of 90 calendar days within the period from the 721st calendar day of precocity.

463. That is why the eventual long period of precocity means a very negative influence on the amount of the old-age pension.

464. The possibility to increase the percentage component of the pension by consideration of insurance period gained during the pension's payment can be applied even here – however, it is related only to the period of insurance period gained after the reach of the statutory retirement age (prior to the reach of retirement age, the overlapping of old-age pension and income from gainful activity is inadmissible in principle).

465. To the day when the beneficiary of 'old-age pension' reaches 100 years of age, the extraordinary supplement to the pension in the amount of CZK 2,000 shall be admitted. From 2019, there is an additional advantageous rule for very old pensioners: from the payment of pension which falls to the calendar month when the beneficiary of 'old-age pension' reaches 85 years of age, the extraordinary supplement to the pension in the amount of CZK 1,000 shall be admitted.

IV. Concurrence of Old-Age Pension with Income from Gainful Activities

466. Since 2010, there are no provisions in legal regulation which would prohibit overlapping of an old-age pension with income from gainful activity in phase *after* the reach of the retirement age. The possibility to earn money besides the enjoying of the old-age pension is, therefore, unlimited in this phase.

467. This applies to the 'regular' pensions as well as to the 'early' pensions. The award of old-age pension or reach of the 'retirement age' is not considered as a statutory reason for an employer's notice to the employee.

468. The only statutory restriction in this regard is related to 'early' old-age pensions which are received in the phase *before* the reach of the retirement age. The payment of this benefit shall not be provided in this phase if the beneficiary simultaneously performs a gainful activity which establishes the participation in pension insurance – in such case, the payment of benefit must be suspended. Such procedure would, however, mean entitlement to increase of the benefit – partial or entire pulling down of the precocity reduction and consideration of additionally gained period of insurance.

§2. Disability (Invalidity) Pensions

469. The invalidity pension represents another type of direct pension benefits granted to persons participating in pension insurance. In special statutory cases, this benefit can also be awarded to a person who did not complete a single day of participation in insurance – this is another expression of outstanding solidarity principle applied in the Czech pension insurance system.

470. The invalidity pension's sense is to compensate for the loss of incomes caused by the 'social event' called invalidity. The 'invalidity' can be defined as a 'partial or full incapacity to perform a gainful activity as a result of the long-term (at least one year according to the medical science's knowledge) unfavourable health status'. In most cases, the invalidity is preceded by the 'TIW' so the payment of invalidity pension comes immediately after the termination of the sickness benefit's payment – the beneficiary is secured continuously.

471. The regulation which was in force prior to the year 2010, differentiated two individual invalidity benefits – 'full' and 'partial' invalidity pension. The abovementioned 'parametric changes' brought a new conception of invalidity pension – a single benefit provided in three amounts depending on the beneficiary's actual stage of invalidity. Once the entitlement to the invalidity pension of any stage arises, it sustains for all the time the invalidity of any stage lasts – by change of the invalidity stage, the amount of benefit changes as well; however, the completion of the required period of insurance is not tested again (as it used to be in the past). This is a very important change which is favourable for the beneficiaries (they do not have to be afraid of the entitlement loss in case of health statuses' change) as well as for the 'social security bodies' (less agenda related to the changes of benefit's amounts).

I. Beneficiaries

472. Provided that the statutory conditions have been complied with, the territorial and personal application to the beneficiaries of invalidity pensions is the same as in the case of old-age pensions.

II. Entitlement Conditions

473. There are several basic entitlement conditions stated by Act on pension insurance.

(1) The person is entitled to the invalidity pension who did not reach 65 years of age and:
   - became invalid in stage one, two or three;
   - completed the 'requested period of insurance';
   - to the day of invalidity's origin did not satisfy the conditions of the entitlement to the 'regular old-age pension';
   - to the day of invalidity's origin did not reach the 'retirement age' if she/he is a beneficiary of the 'early old-age pension'.

(2) Also the person is entitled to the invalidity pension who did not reach 65 years of age and became invalid in stage one, two or three as a result of an 'industrial accident' or of an 'occupational disease' – in such case, the above-mentioned conditions (especially the completion of the 'requested period of insurance') do not have to be satisfied.

474. The person is deemed to be:

- invalid in stage *one* if her/his 'earning ability' has dropped at least by 35% and at most by 49%;
- invalid in stage *two* if her/his 'earning ability' has dropped at least by 50% and at most by 69%;
- invalid in stage *three* if her/his 'earning ability' has dropped at least by 70%.

475. The 'earning ability' means an ability of a person to perform a gainful activity which corresponds to her/his physical, sensual, and psychic abilities with regard to the attained education, experience, knowledge and to the previous gainful activities. The 'drop of the earning activity' means the drop of ability to perform a gainful activity as a result of a limitation of physical, sensual, and psychic abilities as compared to a situation which existed by the person prior to the origin of the 'long-term unfavourable health status'.

476. The assessment of invalidity shall be the matter of the DSSA's physician. The accurate rules for the invalidity's assessing are stated in the Ordinance of the Ministry of Labour and Social Affairs No. 359/2009 Coll.

477. If the entitlement to 'invalidity pension' requires a certain period of insurance, the compliance with this requirement is ascertained in the last decade before the origin of the invalidity. The principal requirement is the insurance period lasting for *five years* – valid for persons who become invalid at the age of 28 years and more. By persons who become invalid in the age of 38 years or more, the condition of the required period of insurance is also satisfied if they had completed *ten years* of insurance in the last two decades before the origin of the invalidity.

478. The required insurance period of the persons who become invalid at the age under 28 is shorter. If they become invalid:

- up to 20 years of age, they need at least one day of insurance;
- from 20 to 22 years of age, they need at least *one year* of insurance;
- from 22 to 24 years of age, they need at least *two years* of insurance;
- from 24 to 26 years of age, they need at least *three years* of insurance;
- from 26 to 28 years of age, they need at least *four years* of insurance.

479. If the person does not comply with the condition of the required insurance period by the day of invalidity's origin, she/he can satisfy it within any ten years after the origin of invalidity. In such a case, however, at least two years of insurance is required even for the persons below 24 years of age.

480. The required insurance period also includes the period of studies at a medium-grade or high-grade school in the Czech Republic and the period for which the person, registered as 'job applicant', receives unemployment benefits (the period during which she/he does not receive unemployment benefits is included up to three years, at the most, and prior to the 55 years of age up to one year, at the most). The condition of at least one year of the 'standard insurance period' does not have to be satisfied for these purposes.

481. The 'third-stage invalidity pension' may also be granted in exceptional cases to a person not complying with the required insurance period. Their number includes the so-called young invalids who had no possibility of being insured because of congenital invalidity or the invalidity acquired during their childhood. Even though the benefit payment in these cases is in conflict with the insurance principle, it solves their difficult social situation. The origin of entitlement to the 'third-stage invalidity pension' requires that the person concerned has attained at least 18 years of age, has a permanent address in the territory of the Czech Republic and is invalid in stage three whereas the invalidity became prior to the age of 18 years.

III. Calculation of Invalidity Pension

482. The invalidity pension consists of the basic part and the percentage-based part.

483. The amount of the *basic part* is determined by an order of the Government. At present (2018), it is CZK 2,700, in 2019 it will be CZK 3,270 per month.

484. The amount of *percentage-based part* is determined, similarly, as by the 'old-age pension' – from the 'calculation base' derived from the mean monthly earnings. The percentage amounts to:

- 1.5% of the calculation base (by the third-stage invalidity pension);
- 0.75% of the calculation base (by the second-stage invalidity pension);

– 0.5% of the calculation base (by the first-stage invalidity pension);

for every completed whole year of the insurance period. The insurance period also includes the so-called 'additional period' which is the period from the origin of the entitlement to the invalidity pension to the attainment of the 'childless woman's retirement age' (appertains also to male pensioners). The percentage-based part of the pension amounts to at least CZK 770.

485. The above-mentioned 'additional period', however, is not included into the calculation of the invalidity pension, if the invalidity has originated by a wilful damage to health which the insured person did himself/herself or caused to be done himself/herself or the damage to health resulting from a wilful criminal offence she/he has committed.

486. The 'additional period' can also be shortened adequately, if the period of time between the day of the eighteenth birthday and the origin of the invalidity is not fully covered by the participation on pension insurance.

487. If the 'third-age invalidity pension' is granted in exceptional cases, the amount of the basic part of the pension is the same and the percentage-based part amounts to 45% of the calculation base which is derived from the 'state average wages'. Since 1 January 2019, the valid 'state average wages' has made CZK 29,979; in 2019 the 'state average wages' will make CZK 32,699.

488. The determination of the invalidity pension's amount, which corresponds to at least 45% of the calculation base derived from the 'state average wages', is also used in cases when:

- the pension's beneficiary is younger than 28 years of age whereas the invalidity originated prior to the age of 18 years or if the period of time between the day of the eighteenth birthday and the origin of the invalidity is fully covered by the participation on pension insurance or if the 'empty period' (period of time without participation in pension insurance) is shorter than one year;
- the pension's beneficiary has completed at least fifteen years of the 'contributory participation' (employment, self-employment, voluntary participation – but not the 'alternative insurance periods').

489. This is valid for the 'third-stage invalidity pensions'; for the 'second-stage invalidity pension', the minimum amount makes half of this amount and for the 'first-stage invalidity pension' the minimum amount makes one-third of this amount.

490. As mentioned above, by the change of the invalidity stage, the amount of benefit changes as well – it increases or drops to the amount which corresponds to the newly assessed stage of invalidity. This process (applied by use of simple rate-coefficient) is very easy in comparison with the procedure applied prior to 2010 (when the completion of the required insurance period was tested again by the change of invalidity stage).

IV. Concurrence of Invalidity Pensions with Income from Gainful Activities

491. If the health status of the invalidity pension's beneficiary permits her/him to perform a gainful activity, the income from this gainful activity has no influence on the payment of pension benefits. Such a person is not even obliged to send to the invalidity pension's payer a notification of such gainful activity's performance.

492. There is only one risk when the beneficiary of the invalidity pension performs a gainful activity – this matter of fact can influence the physician's decision about further existence of the invalidity (concrete stage of invalidity).

493. In the past, the legal regulation stated special rules for the reduction of partial invalidity pension's amount as a result of the parallel performance of a gainful activity. This regulation, however, was derogated in 2006 and, from that time, no limits are applied in this regard.

§3. Survivor's Pensions

494. The pension benefits paid in the Czech Republic, in the case of a bread-winner's death, include the widow's pension, the widower's pension and the orphan's pension. They are indirect pensions derived from the entitlements of the deceased person.

I. Widow's and Widower's Pension

A. *Beneficiaries*

495. The widow's (widower's) pension is due only in the case of husband's (wife's) death and does not apply to the persons living together without the benefit of matrimony. This benefit also does not belong in case of death of the 'registered partner' (registered partnership is to be concluded by persons of the same sex).

B. *Entitlement Conditions*

496. The conditions of entitlement to the widow's and widower's pension are generally identical and depend on the insurance of the deceased.

The widow (widower) is entitled to the widow's (widower's) pension after the death of her/his spouse, who:

- was the beneficiary of old-age pension or of invalidity pension; or
- by the day of her/his death has satisfied the condition of required insurance period to the invalidity pension's entitlement; or
- by the day of her/his death has satisfied the conditions of the entitlement to old-age pension ('regular' or 'early'); or
- died as a result of an industrial accident or an occupational disease.

497. If one of the above-mentioned conditions has been complied with, the widow's (widower's) pension is provided for one year which is always considered the period necessary for the surviving spouse's adaptation to the new situation.

498. After the elapse of one year, the pension entitlement perseveres only if the surviving person complies with, at least, one of the following conditions:

- she/he takes care of an 'unprovided child';
- she/he takes care of a child who is deemed 'dependent on other person's help' in stage II, III or IV (Act No. 108/2006 Coll. on Social Services);
- she/he takes care of her/his parent or the parent of her/his spouse living with her/him in a common household whereas such parent is 'dependent on other person's help' in stage II, III or IV (Act No. 108/2006 Coll. on Social Services);
- she/he is disabled herself/himself in the third stage of invalidity;
- she/he has attained 'statutory age' which is four years lower than makes the 'retirement age' of a male born on the same date as the surviving person (valid also for widows);
- she/he has attained her/his own 'retirement age' if the retirement age is lower than the age determined according to the previous bullet.

499. If the survivor does not comply with one of the above-mentioned conditions for the duration of her/his entitlement after the elapse of one year from her/his spouse' death, her/his entitlement lapses, but originates again, if, at least, one of the above conditions is complied with, within two years from the expiration of the previous entitlement (so-called recovery time). For the widow's (widower's) pensions awarded before 2012, the recovery time is longer and makes five years from the expiration of the previous entitlement.

500. If the widow or widower enters into another matrimony, her/his entitlement to the pension after her/his deceased spouse becomes definitely extinct (without any chance of recovery). From 2012, no smart-money (surrender) is provided any more.

501. According to the present legislation, the entitlement to widow's (widower's) pension lapses (retroactively) also in the case that there is a legally effective judicial decision that the survivor has wilfully caused the death of her/his spouse as a perpetrator of, accomplice to or participant in the criminal act.

C. Calculation

502. These pensions, too, consist of two parts.

503. The basic part amounts to CZK 2,700 (valid for 2018) or CZK 3,270 (valid for the year 2019).

504. The percentage-based part amounts to 50% of the 'old-age pension' or of the 'third-stage invalidity pension' received by the deceased spouse or to which she/he would be entitled at the time of her/his death.

505. By the recovery of the pension, the amount of the new benefit must not be lower than the previous benefit's amount considered to the day of its lapse.

II. Orphan's Pension

A. Beneficiaries

506. Only the unprovided child is entitled to the orphan's pension whose breadwinner (*see* below) has died. The entitlement to orphan's pension does not originate, however, after the death of the foster parent or her/his husband/wife.

B. Entitlement Conditions

507. The orphan's pension is provided in case of the death of:

- the parent; or
- the adoptive parent; or
- the person who took the child into her/his care pursuant to respective judicial decision.

508. The other condition is that the deceased person:

- was the beneficiary of old-age pension or of invalidity pension; or
- by the day of her/his death has satisfied the condition of required insurance period to the invalidity pension's entitlement; from 2012, this condition is considered as satisfied if the deceased person had completed, at least, a half of required insurance period; from February 2018, this condition is considered as satisfied if the deceased person had completed at least one year of 'contributory participation' within the period of ten years before the day of her/his death or (for breadwinners who had died older than 38 years of age) two years of 'contributory participation' within the period of twenty years before the day of her/his death – these are important favours for some orphans; or
- by the day of her/his death has satisfied the conditions of the entitlement to old-age pension ('regular' or 'early'); or

– died as a result of an industrial accident or an occupational disease.

509. If the child's both parents die, such orphan is entitled to orphan's pension after both of them (two individual benefits shall be awarded).

510. The entitlement to orphan's pension lapses by adoption; however, in case of adoption abolition, it is restored again. The entitlement to orphan's pension after the person who took the child into her/his care pursuant to the respective judicial decision also lapses if the child is entrusted to the care of another such person; however, in case of abolition of such care, the pension is restored again.

511. The extinction of the entitlement to orphan's pension is related also to cases when there is a legally effective judicial decision that the orphan had wilfully caused the death of the parent, adoptive parent or the person who has taken the child in her/his care as perpetrator of, accomplice to or participant in the criminal act.

C. Calculation

512. The orphan's pension consists of the basic part and the percentage-based part.

513. The basic part amounts to CZK 2,700 (valid for 2018) or CZK 3,270 (valid for 2019).

514. The percentage-based part amounts to 40% of the 'old-age pension' or the 'third-stage invalidity pension' received by the deceased breadwinner or to which she/he would be entitled at the time of her/his death.

515. By the recovery of the pension, the amount of the new benefit must not be lower than the previous benefit's amount considered to the day of its lapse.

Chapter 2. Pensions for the Self-Employed

516. There are some special rules of the self-employed persons' participation in pension insurance.

§1. Territorial Field of Application

517. The territorial conditions are the same as by the participation in sickness insurance – the self-employment must be carried out in the territory of the Czech Republic or (when the working activity is performed abroad) must be carried out on the basis of licence arising from the Czech legal order.

§2. Personal Field of Application

518. The person is considered as a 'self-employed person' who has terminated compulsory education (basic school) and has reached at least 15 years of age if she/he:

- performs a 'self-employment';
- cooperates by the performance of a 'self-employment' if according to the Income Tax Act (No. 586/1992 Coll.), it is possible to divide the incomes and expenditures of the self-employment to such person.

519. The 'self-employment' is deemed to include:

- the performance of agricultural activities;
- the performance of a small trade (craft) on the basis of a trade certificate;
- the activity of the partner in a public commercial company or the general partner in a limited partnership;
- the performance of art or any other creative activity on the basis of copyright law;
- the performance of any other activities performed outside the labour law relationship on the basis of some authorization (e.g., attorneys-at-law, notaries, tax advisers, judicial experts, interpreters, etc.);
- the performance of other activities performed consistently by the person in their own name and under their own responsibility to produce income (e.g., professional sportsmen); a lease of real property or movables is not considered as the 'self-employment'.

520. The participation in pension insurance is obligatory for the self-employed persons who perform their self-employment as their 'main activity'. In such case, they are always obliged to apply for the participation by the respective DSSA and pay the contributions in an amount determined by themselves (not lower than the statutory minimum – *see* above).

521. The Act on pension insurance, however, also regulates the so-called *adjoining self-employment* where the conditions of participation are not so strict. These persons are not obliged to participate in pension insurance if the incomes (tax base) of such self-employment do not reach the amount of 2.4-multiple of state average wages per year (CZK 71,950 valid for 2018 or CZK 78,478 valid for 2019). If their incomes are lower than this amount, their participation in pension insurance is voluntary only; if they decide for the voluntary participation, they also pay the contributions in an amount determined by themselves (not lower than the statutory minimum – *see* above).

522. 'Adjoining self-employment' is deemed as any gainful activity of a self-employed person in case the person in the year concerned also in parallel:

- performs employment (any of those mentioned in the statutory enumeration above);
- is entitled to receive payment of 'invalidity pension';
- has awarded 'old-age pension' (regular or early);
- is entitled to receive 'parents' allowance' or 'maternity benefit' or 'sickness benefit' because of pregnancy or childbirth;
- takes personal care of another person who is deemed 'dependent on other person's help' according to the special legislation (Act No. 108/2006 Coll. on Social Services) if such dependent person is in 'close relation' to her/him or if the dependent person shares a 'common household' with her/him;
- was considered as an 'unprovided' child (prepares himself/herself for the future profession by studies at a medium-grade or high-grade school).

523. The participation in pension insurance of these persons terminates by the termination of self-employment, its suspension or the extinction of the authorization for its performance.

§3. The Entitlement Conditions and the Calculation Rules

524. The conditions of the origin of entitlement to old-age pension, invalidity pension or survivor's' pensions as well as the rules of their calculation are governed fully by the same regulations as those applicable to the employees and further persons performing working or similar activities (*see* above).

525. Generally, it is possible to say that the pensions of persons who had been participating in pension insurance by reason of performed self-employment are lower (at most) than the pensions of wage-earners. This result is caused by the matter-of-fact that the self-employed persons have a right to determine their calculation base for insurance contributions and that is why they often (in an effort to spare money) set their calculation base in very low amount (this reflects, of course, later in the amount of the pension).

526. In connection with the survivor's' pensions, it is good to remark that in many cases it is difficult for the survivors to gain the entitlement to the pension. The reason why they are not able to gain it is the fact that the self-employed persons often do not perform their duties in the field of pension insurance properly so they are unable to complete the sufficient amount of insurance period to the day of their death. That is probably why the entitlement conditions of the orphan's pension were modified in 2012 and in February 2018 (in order not to leave the orphans concerned unsecured).

Chapter 3. Guaranteed Income for Old Persons

527. The pension insurance system based on the payment of contributions and on the 'insurance principle' cannot solve entirely the problem of poverty of old people. There is no specific legal rule in the Czech Republic guaranteeing the citizens a certain minimum income in their old age. The only provision that can be mentioned herein in connection with pension benefits is the matter-of-fact that the amount of each old-age pension awarded cannot be lower than the minimum amount (i.e., basic component CZK 2,700 plus percentage-based component CZK 770 – valid for 2018; in 2019 the sum of these components shall increase to CZK 4,040 per month).

528. However, this problem is included in the legislation on 'social need' and 'subsistence minimum'.

Part IX. Disabled Persons

529. The approach towards disabled persons in the Czech Republic is slowly changing from a full-care model applied during communist times to a modern approach focused on the integration and social inclusion of people with disabilities, especially through some incentives for employers in order to employ disabled persons and enable them to work as much as possible. Integrating measures also include some incentives and special allowances for service providers who provide special housing for people with disabilities.

530. Last but not least, at the end of 2011, benefits for disabled persons were finally reformed. Originally, these benefits were regulated by a very old and not well-functioning legislation which originated from communist times, and the legislation from the 1980s was still in force. Finally, during 2011, the new Act on benefits for people with disabilities was proposed and adopted. The problem, however, was that it entered into force not even two months after it was adopted. This meant that many offices did not have enough time to prepare themselves properly for such a change (including some technical changes – for example, new software which has to be used in order to provide the benefits to the clients). Right from its beginning, the Act was, therefore, strongly criticized. Some organizations representing people with disabilities also complained that some benefits were reduced through the new system and that especially for severely disabled people, who are not able to work, it is even more difficult to pay for all the services and special treatment which they urgently need. Until today, some difficulties persist; people with some special diagnoses are likely to fall out of the system, as conditions settled by the legislation are not met, even if they might be in serious difficulty. At the same time, the procedure to get some benefits often lasts for too long, so that people have to wait and pay for services from their own pocket.[20]

20. Koldinská, K. Sociální pomoc, in Koldinská, K., Tröster, P. (eds). Právo sociálního zabezpečení. C.H. Beck. Praha, 2018

Chapter 1. Social Integration

531. In the interest of social integration of disabled persons, principal attention concentrates on their employment and on all measures enhancing such employment, particularly their working rehabilitation.

§1. Employment

532. The Charter of Fundamental Rights and Freedoms, which forms part of the constitutional system of the Czech Republic, enshrines the right of the disabled to 'special protection in labour law relations and assistance in their preparation for future profession' (Article 29). The Ministry of Education prepared several amendments to the School Act (Act No. 561/2004 Coll.) in order to reinforce inclusive education available to all pupils with no difference.[21]

533. The Antidiscrimination Act, Act No. 198/2009 Coll., also prohibits discrimination in employment on the ground of disability.

I. Rehabilitation

534. Under Act No. 435/2004 Coll., the right to employment is guaranteed to all citizens, including the disabled if they are able and want to work. In employment mediation, they are entitled to work corresponding to their state of health and the legislation also guarantees them the right to employment corresponding with their working ability, enabling a consistent use of their previous qualification.

535. The employment of the disabled is connected closely with their working rehabilitation, which is deemed to mean consistent care with the purpose of enabling them the performance of their previous or some other suitable job.

536. Working rehabilitation may proceed already at the time the citizen becomes unable to work and includes:

- advisory services in the choice of future profession or other work;
- preparation for future work; and
- provision of employment and the creation of adequate conditions for its performance.

21. This has especially been a reaction to the ECHR judgment *D. H. and Others vs. Czech Republic* from 13.11.2007, app. no. 57325/00

II. Sheltered Workshops

537. The Employment Act also applies to heavily disabled citizens who are employed in sheltered workshops and on sheltered worksites established by their employers. If an employer establishes a sheltered workshop in agreement with the Labour Office of the Czech Republic and undertakes to operate it for at least two years, he can receive a contribution for a person with a health disability to an amount of eight times (in the case of a severely disabled person) or two times (for a disabled person) the average wage within the Czech economy.

538. If the sheltered workshop has been established in agreement with the Labour Office of the Czech Republic, it is also possible to grant a contribution towards their operation which is limited to the amount of three times the average wage within the Czech economy per one disabled employee annually. This contribution is intended to partly cover the operating costs of the sheltered workshop or worksite, in particular, to cover the losses due to lower productivity of disabled employees (e.g., a supplement to the minimum wage), the higher overhead costs of service personnel, medical, social and rehabilitation staff, transport, and so on.

539. The Labour Office of the Czech Republic may grant the above-mentioned level of contribution for the creation of a sheltered worksite and a contribution to partially support transportation also to a disabled job applicant who has decided to work as a self-employed person. However, should he cease performing such work within two years of the date of receiving the said contribution, the Labour Office of the Czech Republic may request for the refund of the sum or a proportionate part thereof. The refund may not be requested if the citizen ceases to perform the said work for reasons of health.

III. Assistance in the Labour Market

540. The Employment Act (Act No. 435/2004 Coll.) provides for support of employers, who establish a workplace for people with disabilities; the Labour Office might cover costs of such a workplace and support an employer with a consultation. For this purpose, the Labour Office and the employer make a written agreement (see Sec. 75-76 of the Employment Act). '

IV. Employment-Supporting Measures

541. Instruments used in the framework of state employment policy for the promotion of the employment of the disabled comprise either economic incentives or administrative measures. A strong instrument is a possibility for an employer who employs people with disabilities to significantly reduce their own income tax base. The tax rate of employers employing more than 50% disabled from the total number of their employees is then further reduced.

542. A positive contribution to the maintenance and possible future increase in the present employment rate of the disabled is provided by the system of subsidies from the state budget. To an employer who employs more than 50% physically disabled persons out of the total number of employees, the Labour Office of the Czech Republic grants a contribution for the support of employment of such persons.

543. Apart from the above-mentioned economic incentives, there are also measures of an administrative character, including obligatory quotas of disabled employees. Every employer who employs more than twenty-five employees has a duty to employ people with disabilities. The obligatory quota is 4% of disabled employees of the total number of employees. Aside from actual employment of disabled persons, employers may satisfy this obligation also by purchasing products or services from special institutions employing more than 50% disabled, by commissioning certain production programmes to these organizations, or buying products of sheltered workshops operated by citizen cooperatives, owned by the state, a church or a religious assembly or by placing orders with these subjects, or buying products or services from self-employed persons with a physical disability. Another way to fulfil the obligation of employing disabled persons is the payment of 2.5 times the average monthly wage within the national economy to the state budget for each person with a physical disability who should be employed. The individual variants may be combined. Should the employer, however, not comply with the imposed obligation through one of these three forms, he would be imposed with a fine.

544. An employer, who welcomes people with disabilities in order to prepare them for work, might get financial support from the Labour Office. The Sec. 72 of the Employment Act defines preparing for work as 'a targeted activity aimed at incorporating a person with disabilities into a suitable job and acquiring the knowledge, skills and habits necessary to perform the chosen job or other gainful activity. This training takes up to 24 months.'

§2. Services

545. Current trends explicitly prefer the disabled to live in a family environment which provides better possibilities for their social integration.

546. Act No. 108/2006 Coll. on social services, regulates social care services provided to people with a certain level of dependency. According to this Act, a person shall be considered dependent on the assistance of another physical person according to four degrees (slight, medium-strong, strong and total dependence), according to their health status as examined by a physician of the DSSA, which narrowly collaborates with the Labour Office of the Czech Republic, and which finally decides on the degree of dependency for the purposes of the care allowance.

547. Social care services are provided as stay-in services, ambulatory services, or field services.

548. There are several types of social care services, defined by the Social Services Act, as follows.

549. Social *care services* assist persons to arrange for their physical and mental self-sufficiency, with the aim of enabling them to integrate into the common social life to the maximum possible extent and, in the case that their health condition excludes such a possibility, to arrange for them a dignified environment and treatment.

550. *Personal assistance* is a field service provided to persons with reduced self-sufficiency due to their age, chronic ailment or disability, where their situation requires the assistance of another physical person. The service is provided without a time limitation, in the natural social environment of a person, and it covers activities needed by a person.

551. *Domiciliary service* is a field or ambulatory service provided to persons with reduced self-sufficiency due to their age, chronic ailment or disability, and to families with children whose situation requires the assistance of another physical person. The service provides the below specific types of assistance in persons' households or in social services facilities at the specified time.

552. *Emergency assistance* is a field service providing non-stop distant vocal and electronic communication with persons exposed to a permanent high risk to health or life in the case of sudden deterioration of their health condition or capacities.

553. *Guiding and reading service* is a field or ambulatory service provided to persons with reduced capacities due to their age or disability in the area of orientation and communication, which assists them in the personal handling of their own matters. Services may also be provided as a part of other services.

554. Supported *housing* is a field service provided to persons with reduced self-sufficiency which is due to a disability or chronic ailment, including mental disorder, and whose situation requires the assistance of another physical person.

555. *Respite care* is a field, ambulatory or stay-in service provided to persons with reduced self-sufficiency due to their age, chronic ailment or disability, for whom the care is given in their natural social environment; the aim of the service being to enable an attending person the necessary rest.

556. In *day services centres*, ambulatory services are provided to persons with reduced self-sufficiency due to their age, chronic ailment or disability, whose situation requires the physical assistance of another person. In *daycare centres*, ambulatory services are provided to persons with reduced self-sufficiency due to their age or disability, and to persons with a chronic mental disorder, whose situation requires regular physical assistance from another person. In *week care centres*, stay-in services are provided to persons with reduced self-sufficiency due to their age or disability, and to persons with a chronic mental disorder, whose situation requires the regular physical assistance of another person.

557. In *homes for disabled persons*, stay-in services shall be provided to persons with reduced self-sufficiency due to their disability, whose situation requires the regular physical assistance of another person.

558. In special *regime homes*, stay-in services are provided to persons with reduced self-sufficiency due to a chronic mental disorder or dependence on addictive substances, and to persons with old-age/senile dementia, Alzheimer's disease and other types of dementia with reduced self-sufficiency due to the respective disorder, whose situation requires the regular physical assistance of another person. When providing services, the regime within these facilities is adjusted to the specific needs of these persons.

559. *Protected housing* is an ambulatory service provided to persons with reduced self-sufficiency due to their disability or chronic disease, including mental disorders, whose situation requires the physical assistance of another person. Protected housing takes the form of group, or possibly individual, housing.

560. In *healthcare residential facilities*, stay-in social services are provided to persons no longer requiring stay-in healthcare, who are, however, unable to live without the physical assistance of another person due to their health condition and who, thus, cannot be released from healthcare residential facilities until assistance is arranged for them through a close person or another person, or until the provision of field or ambulatory social services or stay-in social services within social services facilities is arranged for them.

§3. Environment Accessibility

561. The requirements concerning environment accessibility concern, generally, residential buildings and newly erected or reconstructed public buildings, means of public transportation, streets and other external environments.

562. Possibilities offered to the disabled in the field of housing include, for example, modification of their existing flat. As a rule, this includes the elimination of barriers (installation of a lift, modification of doors and the interior), the installation of sound or light signals, and so on.

563. Regulations concerning the accessibility of public buildings for the disabled form part of the Building Act. The Act instructs the Building Authority to assess 'whether the design satisfies the general technical requirements ensuring the use of the building by the persons with limited possibility of movement and orientation'. If the design does not satisfy these requirements, it must not be approved.

Apart from buildings with flats, this criterion is also applied to buildings for administration and management, services, trade and public catering, physical education, education, culture, health services, social care, public transportation and temporary accommodation (hostels, dormitories, hotels, etc.).

§4. Education and Training

564. The priority respected in this field consists of the principle of equal opportunity of access to elementary, secondary and higher education in an integrated environment, if possible, for disabled children, juveniles and adults.

565. The present legislation concerning the education and training of juveniles contained in the Education Act (Act No. 561/2004 Coll.) is satisfactory in this respect. It provides, for example, the deaf and the blind with the right to education in their own language using sign language or Braille and free interpreting services.

566. The Education Act prefers integrated education. However, if disabled persons cannot be educated together with other pupils, their education and training are provided for in special schools. These are special elementary and secondary (medium-grade) schools providing education equivalent to standard schools. The Czech Republic has been criticized for many years, as these schools, which were originally intended for pupils with mental disorders, have been very much used for Roma children who are healthy, but due to their social exclusion are not able to keep up at regular schools, especially during the first years of education if not specially guided or assisted in classes (*see also* the famous judgment of the ECHR in *D.H. and Others v. Czech Republic*). Especially nowadays, the Czech Republic is working on improving the level of inclusive education.[22]

567. The state of health of the child is taken into account also by some state social support benefits in which the state participates in covering the costs of sustenance and other fundamental personal necessities of families with children. Under Act No. 117/1995 Coll., there are more relaxed income conditions for families with disabled children claiming certain income-tested benefits.

---

22. *See, e.g.*, Koldinská, K. Right to education – a case of Roma children in Central Europe, in Devetzi, S., Janda, C. 'Sicherheit – Gerechtigkeit – Sozial(es) Recht', Nomos Verlag, 2015.

Chapter 2. Financial Allowances for the Disabled

568. As of 1 January 2012, financial allowances for the disabled are regulated in Act No. 329/2011 Coll. on providing benefits to persons with disabilities.

§1. Beneficiaries

569. According to the above-mentioned Act, beneficiaries from the benefits are people with disabilities, who reside permanently in the territory of the Czech Republic, or foreigners who have been entitled to special international protection, or any citizen of a Member State of the EU, and her/his family member, who resides on the territory of the Czech Republic.

570. The health conditions of disabled persons are examined by specialists of the DSSA.

§2. Conditions

571. There are two basic benefits which can be claimed within the system of benefits to persons with disabilities.

572. Entitled to mobility allowance are persons older than one year who are not able to fulfil their own basic life needs in the area of mobility and orientation, who regularly have to travel or be transported, and who are not the client of any residential services under the Act on Social Services (*see* section 6 of Act No. 329/2011 Coll.).

573. According to section 9 of Act No. 329/2011 Coll., entitlement to the allowance for a special aid instrument arises for a person with a heavy disability in moving or heavy disability in hearing or seeing if the health situation of such person equates to a long-lasting non-beneficiary health condition. Furthermore, the aid instrument shall make auto sufficiency possible to an entitled person or is needed to enable such a person to work, to study, or to be in contact with others.

§3. Benefits

574. As already mentioned, there are two benefits:

- mobility allowance; and
- allowance for a special aid instrument.

575. Mobility allowance is paid especially in order to contribute to travel expenses for a person with a disability. The amount of such an allowance is CZK 550 per month.

576. An allowance for a special aid instrument is more variable and is provided in order to enable social inclusion for a person with a disability. The allowance is paid to purchase always only a basic alternative to an aid instrument. It is possible also to use the allowance, for example, to buy a car or a guide dog for the blind.

577. There is an income test for aid instruments which are not so expensive. If the price of the aid instrument is lower than CZK 24,000, the allowance is provided only if the income of the claimant and of persons whose income is counted together is lower than eighteen times their subsistence minimum. The allowance is provided always so that the person with the disability contributes 10% from their own money, at a minimum CZK 1,000. The maximum amount of the allowance is CZK 350,000; if it's a lifting platform, it's CZK 400,000. The total amount of allowance cannot exceed CZK 800,000.

578. The person for whom an aid instrument has been provided must return it back in its whole amount or in an adequate amount if the allowance is not used within three months from the day on which it was provided, or if it is not used in the whole amount provided. In the case of an allowance provided to buy a car, it must be returned if within 84 months the person ceases to be the owner of the respective car (the limit is sixty months if the aid instrument is not a car – for example, if it was a computer for blind persons).

579. The RBLO have to decide on both allowances.

Part X. Minimum Income Benefit

580. The Charter of Fundamental Rights and Freedoms, forming part of the constitutional system of the Czech Republic, guarantees to everyone who is in material need the right to such assistance as is essential for the assurance of her/his basic living conditions (Article 30).

581. The most important act which implements this fundamental right is Act No. 111/2006 Coll. on assistance in material need. This Act regulates a modern system to assist those with insufficient income; the system motivates them to actively strive to secure the resources they need to meet their living requirements. It is one of the means applied by the Czech Republic to combat social exclusion. The Act, as a whole, is based on the principle that 'all persons who work must be better off than those who are out of work or who avoid work'.

582. The Act on Assistance in Material Need lays down situations of inadequate means of subsistence or housing and defines some emergencies. The system helps to deal with certain special circumstances that can only be resolved with immediate assistance. The Act sets the rule that everyone is entitled to receive basic information that cannot only address their particular material need but also, in the first place, prevent it from occurring. Social work with clients is an integral part of the system of assistance in material need.

583. The system has been recently strongly discussed, as, in the Czech Republic, there are many socially excluded localities, where people live in housing of a very low standard, but have to pay a very high rent. This rent is paid by the system of social assistance, directly to private owners of these houses. This situation is caused by many factors, including the fact that many local authorities, in the first half of the 1990s, sold their properties and so there is currently a lack of social housing for poor people, which should be provided by municipalities.

Chapter 1. Beneficiaries

584. Act No. 111/2006 Coll. defines a person in material need as a beneficiary of the system, as a person or family that does not have enough income where their overall social and property relations prevent them from enjoying what society accepts to be basic living requirements. At the same time, these persons are objectively unable to increase their income (through the due application of entitlement and claims or through the sale or other disposals of their own assets), thereby improving their situation through their own actions.

585. There is also a negative legislative definition of a person in material need. Persons who are not deemed to be persons in material need are those who do not try to improve their situation by their own actions, who are not in an employment or similar relationship, are not self-employed or not listed in the register of job seekers, who are listed in the register of job seekers and who have refused to take up short-term employment or to participate in an active employment policy programme without serious reason, who are not entitled to sickness benefit or who have been awarded a reduced level of benefit because they intentionally brought about their illness, who are self-employed and their income, after the deduction of reasonable housing costs, is lower than the amount of living due to the fact that they were not enrolled in sickness insurance, who have been sanctioned for failing to comply with their obligations as a child's legal representative connected with the truancy of the child (during the time of compulsory school attendance), or who are in preventive detention or in remand (for a full calendar month).

Chapter 2. Conditions

586. Benefits provided under the system of assistance in material need are:

- Allowance for Living.
- Supplement for Housing.
- Extraordinary Immediate Assistance.

587. Allowance for Living is the basic benefit covering cases of material need that tackles the insufficient income of a person or family. Persons or families are entitled to an allowance for a living if the income of these persons or families is less than the amount of living when reasonable housing costs have been deducted.

588. The amount of living is established on a case-by-case basis, based on an evaluation of the person's income, efforts and opportunities. The amount of living for families is determined by the sum of the amounts of living of each family member. The amount of living is derived from the existence minimum and the subsistence minimum. The amount of living for a person, who owes maintenance to a child at an amount exceeding three monthly payments, is the amount of the existence minimum, eventually increased due to the need of special, e.g., dietary food, which is normally much more expensive than regular alimentation. The amount of living for a person, who is listed in the register of job seekers and whose employment was terminated due to infringement of labour law rules in the last six months prior to the submission of an application for a benefit is the amount of the existence minimum, eventually increased due to dietary food. The amount of living for a person who is undergoing healthcare in a health facility for a full calendar month is the amount of the existence minimum, eventually increased due to dietary food.

589. Supplement for Housing tackles cases where the income of the person or family, including entitlement to a housing allowance from the system of state social support, is insufficient to cover justified housing costs.

590. The benefit is provided to flat owners or tenants who are entitled to an allowance for living and a housing allowance. In exceptional cases, a supplement for housing can be provided to a person not eligible for a housing allowance or to a person using a form of housing other than the rental.

591. The period of the benefit's payment is limited to eighty-four months within the last ten calendar years. An exception applies to households exclusively consisting of people over 70 years and disabled persons living in flats adjusted for them.

592. The legislation has been recently amended in order to reduce the socially excluded localities, or better said, in order not to support newcomers and so not to extend ghettos. Act No. 111/2006 Coll. currently states that people, who come new to the socially excluded locality, shall not be entitled to supplement for housing. Municipalities are entitled to declare their territories as socially excluded localities.

Using this possibility, there is even one whole city, which declared its whole territory as socially excluded locality. This legislation has been put before the Constitutional Court, with support of the Public Defender of Rights.[23]

593. *Extraordinary Immediate Assistance* is provided to persons who find themselves in situations that have to be resolved immediately. The Act addresses six situations that justify this benefit as follows.

594. Where persons do not meet the conditions of material need but, due to a lack of funds, suffer from a serious threat to their health. The benefit tops up a person's income so that it is level with the existence minimum (or the subsistence minimum in cases of dependent children).

595. Where persons are victims of a serious extraordinary event (a natural disaster, storms and gales, ecological disasters, fire, etc.). The maximum amount of the benefit is fifteen times the individual's subsistence minimum, i.e., up to CZK 51,150.

596. Where persons do not have enough resources to cover essential one-off expenditure connected, in particular, with the payment of an administrative fee for duplicate copies of personal documents or in cases of monetary loss. The maximum amount of the benefit is the amount of this one-off expenditure.

597. Where persons do not have enough resources to acquire or repair basic furniture or durables: The maximum amount of the benefit is the amount of this expenditure, but the sum of benefits granted must not exceed ten times the individual's subsistence minimum in one calendar year.

598. Where persons do not have enough resources to cover justified costs relating to the education or special interests of dependent children or ensuring necessary activities concerning the social and legal protection of children: The amount of the benefit may be a maximum of the specific expense, but the sum of benefits granted must not exceed ten times the individual's subsistence minimum in one calendar year.

599. Where persons are at risk of social exclusion: This concerns, for example, the situation of persons who have been released from custody or from prison, who have left an orphanage or foster care on reaching adulthood, or who have completed treatment for addiction. A benefit of up to CZK 1,000 may be granted. The benefit may be awarded repeatedly, but the sum of benefits granted in one calendar year may not exceed four times the individual's subsistence minimum.

600. For the sake of being thorough, we can also mention the *housing allowance*, which is an income-tested benefit provided within the state social support system.

---

23. Pending case Pl. ÚS 40/17.

601. Property owners or tenants registered as permanently resident in that property are entitled to a housing allowance if 30% (in Prague 35%) of family income is insufficient to cover housing costs and at the same time this 30% (in Prague 35%) of family income is lower than the relevant prescriptive costs set by law.

602. The prescriptive housing costs are set as average housing costs based on the size of the municipality and the number of members of the household. In the case of rented flats, they include a proportion of the rent in accordance with the Rent Act and similar costs for residents of cooperative flats and flat owners. They also include the cost of services and energy. Prescriptive housing costs are calculated on the basis of reasonable sizes of flats for the number of persons permanently residing in them.

603. The level of housing allowance is set as the difference between prescriptive housing costs and the relevant family income, multiplied by a coefficient of 0.30 (in Prague 0.35).

604. The period of a benefit's payment is limited to eighty-four months within the last ten calendar years. An exception applies to households consisting exclusively of people over 70 years and disabled persons living in flats adjusted for them.

Chapter 3. Amount of the Benefit

605. The amount of the allowance for a living is set as the difference between the amount of living of a person or family and the income of that person or family, less reasonable housing costs. (Reasonable housing costs are the cost of housing to a maximum of 30%, in Prague 35%, of the income of the person or family).

606. The amount of the supplement for housing is determined in such a manner that, on payment of justified housing costs (i.e., rent, services related to housing and energy costs), the person or family is left with the amount of living.

607. The amount of extraordinary immediate assistance differs according to concrete cases, as explained above.

Chapter 4. Claims and Administration

608. RBLO are responsible for granting and disbursing benefits in material need.

609. The proceedings start after an application on a prescribed form is submitted.

610. Applications for benefits are submitted to the competent RBLO according to the applicant's permanent residence.

611. A decision to grant benefits assesses whether the person or family is actually in material need and whether they comply with the conditions for that particular benefit. In the final phase, the level of benefit is determined. The Uniform Information System of Labour and Social Affairs ensures an integrated approach throughout the territory of the Czech Republic.

Chapter 5. Reclaiming of Benefits Paid

612. A beneficiary who has not fulfilled any of his duties and has been receiving a benefit, although he must have known or assumed from the circumstances that it was paid without entitlement or at a higher rate than due or who has caused such a situation wilfully himself/herself, is obliged to refund the benefits accruing from the day from which she/he was not entitled to them. This applies particularly to cases where she/he has not fulfilled her/his notification duty, has been receiving the benefit under false pretences or has failed to disclose some decisive fact or circumstance.

613. The obligation to refund benefits received without entitlement or in an incorrect amount is decided by the authority who granted them.

614. A claim for the refund of the benefit granted without entitlement or in an incorrect amount expires with the lapse of three years from the day on which the appropriate authority ascertained the fact, at the latest, however, with the lapse of ten years from the day from which the benefit has been paid. These terms are stayed for the period of remedial proceedings, execution of the decision and for the period during which instalments for the refund of excessive payment are deducted from the benefits.

Part XI. Claims and Adjudication

615. The whole part of claims and adjudication within the social security field is in general governed by the Act on Administrative Procedure and by the Act on Judicial Administrative Procedure, as explained above in the introductory part to this study.

616. Specific provisions are regulated in specific acts on respective systems of social security.

Chapter 1. Claims

§1. Introduction of Claims

617. The claim is in most cases presented through a written claim submitted on a prescribed form.

618. For the purposes of pension insurance, for example, there is a specific procedure to introduce the claim. In the case of old-age pensions, the submission of the pension application is preceded by a preliminary procedure intended to inform the prospective claimant about the insurance (employment) periods recorded in the files of the CSSA. In this way, the claimant (applicant) learns on time which insurance periods he has to prove himself/herself in her/his own interest because they are not recorded in central files. It is the duty of the employer to request, on behalf of his employees, a statement of recorded insurance periods two years at the earliest and one year at the latest before the year in which the citizen attains the statutory retirement age. The statement is sent directly to the citizen who encloses it with his pension application.

619. The pension application is drafted by the District (or Prague, as the case may be) Social Insurance Administration. Within eight days after its drafting, this application is submitted to the DSSA.

§2. Protection Against Seizure and Transfer

620. In general, social benefits cannot be subject to any seizure or transfer, including the executions according to civil procedure.

621. The Pension Insurance Act (Act No. 155/1995 Coll.), for example, enables regular deductions from a pension on the basis of an agreement. Such agreement, however, may be concluded only in the case of alimony, contribution to sustenance and the refund of pension overpayments, and it may amount only to the sum which may be deducted in the execution of the decision.

622. The fundamental amount which may not be touched at the time of execution of the decision is determined by Order of the Government No. 63/1998 Coll. This amount equals 62% of the subsistence minimum of the liable person and 25% of the subsistence minimum for each person to whom the liable person is obliged to provide sustenance, including the husband or wife.

§3. Legal Capacity to Receive Benefits

623. Legal capacity to receive benefits differs from one system to the other, depending on its functions. In general, legal capacity to receive a benefit starts with birth (e.g., in the case of healthcare, some state social support benefits) or when the person reaches 18 years of age (e.g., pensions). In the case of sickness insurance, the person can be insured and, thus, receive benefits after she/he reaches 15 years of age and finishes obligatory school attendance (section 5 of the Act No. 187/2006 Coll. on sickness insurance, section 6 of the Labour Code and section 34 of the Civil Code).

Chapter 2. Adjudication

624. A proposal for judicial review can be submitted to an administrative court under certain conditions. The proposal for judicial review usually has no dilatory effect.

625. Courts never review decisions on applications for the mitigation of undue hardships of the law. These hardships may be mitigated only by the Minister of Labour and Social Affairs.

626. A court decides on a proposal for judicial review submitted in due time and showing no defects either by confirming the contested decision as correct and legal or by quashing it and returning it for the further procedure (cassation). If the decision has been quashed, the office which decided in the first instance is bound to respect the opinion of the court in the resumed proceedings.

627. The court is not authorized to decide directly about the benefit itself; it merely reviews the legality of the contested decision.

628. Appeal against the decision of a court may be submitted to the Supreme Administrative Court.

629. Cases implying the jurisdiction of courts in decisions on social security matters are decided by general civil courts in accordance with the provisions of Act No. 150/2002 Coll. on Rules of Administrative Judiciary because there are no specialized courts for this field in the Czech Republic. In proceedings on all matters concerning social insurance, the courts act as reviewing or appellate institutions. As it follows from the preceding chapter, decisions on applications are made, in the first instance, by administrative bodies governed by the Rules of Administrative Procedure, unless the law provides differently. In the course of judicial review, the procedure is ensured by courts of a higher level. In relation to matters concerning cases of remedy against effective decisions of courts of a higher level, it is the Supreme Administrative Court that decides on cassation appeals.

630. The principle of free evaluation of evidence is applied in proceedings before the issue of the decision. The insurance agency assesses the collected evidence both separately and in mutual relations. In some proceedings, however, the legislation requires in some cases the provision of concrete proof (so-called obligatory proof) in connection with proving certain facts.

Selected Bibliography

Boučková, P., et al. Anditidiskriminační zákon – komentář. C.H. Beck. 2016.

Břeská, N., E. Burdová & L. Vránová. Státní sociální podpora. Olomouc: ANAG, 2012.

Červinka, T. Zdravotní pojištění zaměstnavatelů, zaměstnanců a OSVČ s komentářem a příklady 2012. Olomouc: ANAG, 2012.

Koldinská, K. & I. Tomeš. *Integration into Work of Persons Who Were Already Disabled Before Adulthood*. National Report in National Report Czech Republic. Tilburg – OSA: Institute for Labour Studies, 2008.

Koldinská, K. (ed.): Sociální zabezpečení migrujících osob. Praha: C.H. Beck, 2010.

Koldinská, K. 'EU-Compatible Interpretation of the National Law with Some Constitutional Reservations Case of the Czech Republic'. In *European Legal Method – Paradoxes and Revitalisation*, edited by U. Neergaard, R. Nielsen & L. Roseberry. Haaftet: Nyhed, 2011.

Koldinská, K. Gender a sociální právo (Gender and social law). Praha: C.H. Beck, 2010.

Koldinská, K. 'Should Fathers Not Raise Their Children? Two Cases of ECHR and ECJ on Gender Equality in Pensions Rights'. *European Gender Equality Law Review* 2 (2011), available at http://ec.europa.eu/justice/gender-equality/files/egelr__2011-2_en.pdf.

Koldinská, K. Sociální právo. Praha: C.H. Beck, 2013.

Koldinská, K. & M. Štefko (eds). *Reflections on 20 Years of Social Reform in Central and Eastern Europe*. Auditorium: Praha, 2010.

Koldinská, K. & I. Tomeš. Právní a organizační aspekty posuzování zdravotního stavu v sociální oblasti. Univerzita Karlova v Praze, Právnická fakluta, ediční středisko, Praha, 2011.

Lang, R. Důchody poskytované invalidním osobám od roku 2010, Personální a sociálněprávní kartotéka (02/2011). Praha: Linde, 2011.

Lang, R. & J. Pilařová. Vdovské a vdovecké důchody od 1.1.2010, Personální a sociálněprávní kartotéka (02/2010). Praha: Linde, 2010.

Lang, R. Vliv nezaměstnanosti na budoucí důchodové nároky jedince, Personální a sociálněprávní kartotéka (01/2010). Praha: Linde, 2010.

Lang, R. Výkon výdělečné činnosti v souběhu s pobíráním důchodu v roce 2010, Personální a sociálněprávní kartotéka (05/2010). Praha: Linde, 2010.

Přib, J. K nálezu Ústavního soudu k výpočtu důchodů, Personální a sociálněprávní kartotéka (06/2010). Praha: Linde, 2010.

Selected Bibliography

Přib, J. & V. Voříšek. Důchodové předpisy s komentářem. Olomouc: ANAG, 2012.

Tomeš, I. (ed.). Sociální správa. Praha: Portál, 2009.

Koldinská, K., Tomeš, I., Křepelka, F. Sociální právo Evropské unie. Prague: Wot-ers Kluwer, 2017.

Koldinská, K., Tröster, P., et al. Právo sociálního zabezpečení. Prague: C.H. Beck, 2018.

Ženíšková, M. & J. Přib. Zákon o nemocenském pojištění s komentářem a příklady od 1.1.2016. Olomouc ANAG, 2016.

Ženíšková, M. Pojistné na sociální zabezpečení s komentářem a příklady k 1. 1. 2016. Olomouc ANAG, 2016.

Index

The numbers here refer to paragraph numbers.

Index

Index

Made in the USA
Monee, IL
18 October 2026

66041390R10109